Quick & Simple Air Fryer Cookbook
© 2023 Future Publishing Limited

Future Books is an imprint of Future PLC
Quay House, The Ambury, Bath, BA1 1UA

All contents © 2023 Future Publishing Limited or published under licence. All rights reserved. No part of this title may be used, stored, transmitted or reproduced in any way without the prior written permission of the publisher. Future Publishing Limited (company number 2008885) is registered in England and Wales. Registered office: Quay House, The Ambury, Bath BA1 1UA. All information contained in this publication is for information only and is, as far as we are aware, correct at the time of going to press.

A catalogue record for this book is available from the British Library.

ISBN 9781805211686 hardback

The paper holds full FSC certification and accreditation.

Printed in Italy by Elcograf, for Future PLC

Editors
Jane Curran and Zara Gaspar
Deputy Food Editor
Rose Fooks
Group Food Director
Jen Bedloe
Senior Art Editor
Andy Downes
Head of Art & Design
Greg Whitaker
Editorial Director
Jon White
Managing Director
Grainne McKenna
SVP Lifestyle, Knowledge and News
Sophie Wybrew-Bond
Production Project Manager
Matthew Eglinton
Global Business Development Manager
Jennifer Smith
Head of Future International & Bookazines
Tim Mathers

Cover images
FUTURECONTENTHUB.COM
Chris Alack, Jen Bedloe (food styling)
and Victoria Eldridge (prop styling)

FUTURE
Connectors.
Creators.
Experience
Makers.

Future plc is a public company quoted on the London Stock Exchange (symbol: FUTR) www.futureplc.com

Chief Executive Officer **Jon Steinberg**
Non-Executive Chairman **Richard Huntingford**
Chief Financial and Strategy Officer **Penny Ladkin-Brand**

Tel +44 (0)1225 442 244

Quick & Simple
AIR FRYER
COOKBOOK

Welcome...

Air fryers have become a must-have in the modern kitchen, and everyone's jumping on the trend. So we've packed this book with recipes for delicious snacks, easy sides, must-make mains and simple sweet treats.

Read our tips on choosing an air fryer, what's great to cook in it, and what isn't. It's perfect for small roasts, with no large oven to clean. Of course, anything you'd normally fry, such as fries or chicken nuggets, gives a perfect result without all the oil, so your calorie count will thank you.

How does it work? It doesn't technically fry anything, but has heat which radiates from a heating element, with a powerful fan to circulate the hot air – hence it works like a convection oven. So think of your air fryer as a mini convection oven, which heats much faster than a conventional oven, and which may help to save on energy bills. From cold, most models will be at the correct temperature in under three minutes, whereas a standard oven will be over ten minutes, if not more. It will definitely save time, and you'll be amazed at how versatile it is. There is a huge choice out there – some are combined with a pressure cooker, some have two drawers to cook different foods at the same time, others have a large, single drawer. All you need is sufficient space on your work surface, with a little space behind to keep the fan clear and circulating. You'll soon discover it's a master for re-heating food. Much as we love a microwave, an air fryer will reheat a slice of quiche or pizza until crisp and crunchy, which a microwave will fail to do.

From the simplest ideas to stunning soufflés, make your air fryer work for you. And it's easy enough to get the kids involved, too, which can only be a bonus!

CONTENTS

p10 — Top 10 air fryer tips to master the art!

64

92

111

59

26

157

Sides

Something Sweet

TOP 10
Air fryer tips

Master the art of air-frying with our quick essential guide

1 HELPFUL KIT

Some recipes need the use of a liner, either silicone or pierced parchment paper. These are sold specifically for air fryers and are pretty much the perfect size. Use them to save messing up the main drawer, but it's also handy when air-frying sticky bakes, cookies and foods. The less washing-up, the better, in our book. An oil spray is also useful. Ramekin dishes, silicone muffin cases and small gratin dishes which fit easily into the drawer will be perfect for muffins, crumbles and reheating. A 18cm (7in) round or 15cm (6in) square cake tin is just what you need for flapjacks and brownies. It's amazing how creative you can be with kit for the air fryer. Ready-made baking parchment cake tin liners are handy for granola or toasting nuts and seeds. Small metal pudding basins (sometimes called dariole moulds) come in handy for mini cakes and baked desserts.

2 DON'T OVERFILL

The powerful fan makes the air circulate evenly, so there are no hot or cold spots in an air fryer. But do ensure foods have space around them, to allow for even cooking and for the air to circulate. Avoid stacking up any foods, which will just become soggy, instead of light and crisp. Cook in batches if you need to – the air fryer is a whiz at re-heating foods.

3 AVOID SAUCES

Best to leave saucy dishes to a conventional oven or microwave. In an air fryer, the sauce will bubble, may splatter and hit the heating element. This could smoke or cause damage to the element. But by all means, bake your meatballs for spaghetti in the air fryer first, before adding them to the hot sauce.

4 BATTER IS A NO-NO

When deep-frying battered foods, the batter solidifies as soon as it hits the hot oil, not the case with an air fryer. The batter will drip through the basket and cause damage. So stick with crumbed foods instead.

5 DRY RUBS ARE BETTER THAN WET

Like cooking sauced dishes, anything too wet will drip through the basket and mess up the air fryer. It may cause damage. But dry rubs and marinades are simply perfect. Try rubbing a chicken for roasting with a blend of salt, sugar, lemon zest, chilli powder and ground coriander seeds. If there's a recipe which uses a marinade as a baste, this is fine to brush on halfway through cooking.

6 WHEN TO SPRAY

Spritz or coat foods in oil before they go into the air fryer. Most crumbed foods benefit from a spray to achieve that gorgeous, golden crumb. Vegetables for roasting, especially broccoli and cauliflower, benefit from a good coating of oil to prevent them drying out. Any filled pastries with an egg wash are fine, too – just brush the top, air fry, then turn halfway and brush with the egg wash again.

7 LIGHT FOODS

By "light", we mean weight, so think popcorn for starters. The fan will just blow the popcorn around, causing it to jump into the heating element and a possible fire hazard. Similarly if you're baking a pizza with pepperoni, it will just fly off. However, if you put the pepperoni beneath a slice of mozzarella, it will pin it down! To melt cheese, on a burger for example, wait until the timer has finished, but the air fryer is still hot, then add your cheese to melt once the fan has stopped. Otherwise the fan will blow off a piece of sliced cheese and make for painful washing up.

8 HOW TO CLEAN

The baskets of most air fryers are dishwasher proof, though they only take a few minutes to clean in hot, soapy water. Avoid any abrasive scourers, which will remove the non-stick element. Allow the basket to cool before washing, but clean while it's still warm for ease. Wipe out the interior and clean the exterior with a hot, soapy cloth. Remember there needs to be space behind the air fryer, where the external panel of the fan is ventilated. Avoid putting it too close to the kitchen wall, leaving space behind. The fat generated may mark the wall or tiles, so give it a good wipe with a damp, soapy cloth after use.

9 TIMINGS & SHAKES

Most recipes will benefit from a shake of the air fryer basket now and again through cooking. We give instructions when to do so in our recipes, but as a general rule, shake the basket halfway through cooking for vegetables, fries and nuggets. Some recipes ask for the food to be turned halfway through also, for even cooking. It's also important to bear in mind that, just as a conventional oven, timings on an air fryer may vary slightly, according to the brand. So it may be a minute less or more here and there. You'll become more proficient with practice. Some air fryers also have rather odd temperature displays, so yours may show at 402°F, rather than 400°F. But frankly, that's not going to make a huge difference – just trust your judgment. As a general rule, foods will take 20% less time and at 20-30% a lower temperature than a conventional oven, though it will depend on your air fryer and on the recipe.

10 WATCH OUT FOR THE HEATING ELEMENT

It's very important to avoid any food stuffs touching the element above the air fryer basket, which could cause a fire hazard or damage the element. This particularly applies to whole chickens or joints of meat. As you get used to your air fryer, you'll be a better judge on the correct size to buy. Usually, a piece of meat or chicken weighing around 1kg (2 1/4lb) will be the perfect fit.

Practice makes perfect!

Air-frying is really straightforward and simple. With a little practice, you'll get to know your favourite dishes and snacks to make. Think of it as an extension to your conventional oven and fryer, and you'll be amazed at how versatile it is.

LIGHT BITES & SNACKS

Make the best ever spicy little dumplings – better than a takeaway!

Chicken murtabaks

These lightly-spiced filo triangles are so quick to air fry. If baking from frozen, add an extra 2-3 minutes to the initial cooking time and double check they are fully heated through before serving.

Makes 48 • Ready in 45 minutes

- 4tbsp dried tamarind, broken up
- 500g (1lb 2oz) chicken breast fillets, finely chopped
- 4 garlic cloves, peeled and crushed
- 75g (3oz) ginger, peeled and shredded
- 50g (2oz) raisins or sultanas
- 85g (3½oz) pine nuts, toasted
- 2tsp five-spice powder
- 2tsp ground turmeric
- 1tsp salt
- 6tbsp coconut cream
- 25g (1oz) chopped coriander leaves

For the pastry
- 250g (9oz) filo pastry sheets
- 150g (5oz) ghee or butter, melted

1 Place the tamarind in a heatproof jug and cover with 300ml (½pt) boiling water. Stir, cover and microwave on high for 3 minutes. Mash and stir with a fork, then discard the seeds. Transfer 3tbsp of the pulp to a bowl and mix with the remaining filling ingredients. Set aside to marinate.
2 Cut 12 pastry sheets lengthways into 4 equal-sized strips, around 8-10cm (3-4in) wide. Place in 2 piles and cover with a damp tea towel to prevent the pastry drying out. Brush the first strip with ghee. Spoon a walnut-sized portion of filling on the top left corner. Starting from this corner, fold the pastry diagonally, over and over, to form a triangle, and brush with a little more ghee. Repeat until all the ingredients have been used up.
3 Heat the air fryer to 180°C/350°F. Air fry the filo triangles in batches for 4 minutes, turning halfway through, then increase the heat to 200°C/400°F and bake for 2 minutes, until browned and crispy.

Warm roast carrot, chickpea & spinach salad with a tahini dressing

These carrots are so sweet. You could also toss the chickpeas in a little olive oil and salt, then air fry them at 200°C/400°F for 5 minutes until crisp, shaking a few times during cooking.

Serves 4 • Ready in 20 minutes

- **500g (1lb 2oz) baby carrots, scrubbed, fronds trimmed**
- **2 tbsp olive oil**
- **½ - 1tsp dried chilli flakes, to taste**
- **1½ tsp cumin seeds**
- **1tsp hot smoked paprika**
- **1tbsp soft brown sugar**
- **100g (3 ½oz) baby spinach leaves**
- **2 tins chickpeas, drained and rinsed**

For the dressing:
- **2 tbsp tahini paste**
- **1 garlic clove, crushed**
- **1tsp honey**
- **2tbsp extra virgin olive oil**
- **Squeeze of lemon juice**

1 Toss the carrots with the olive oil, chilli flakes, cumin, half the paprika, the sugar and salt and pepper. Heat the air fryer to 200°C/400°F. Air fry the carrots for 12 minutes, shaking them half way through. Cool slightly and divide between plates with the spinach leaves and chickpeas. Sprinkle with the remaining paprika.
2 To make the dressing, stir the tahini before measuring. Whisk the ingredients together with 4 tablespoons cold water and season to taste. Thin with a little more water if it seems too thick; it should have the consistency of double cream. Spoon over the salad in ribbons and serve.

Tortilla chips with party guacamole

Air fryer chips are ready in minutes. Tequila adds a subtle kick to this creamy dip – give it a shot!

Serves 6 • Ready in 20 minutes

- 12 tortillas or flatbreads
- Olive oil spray
- Sea salt
- 4 avocados
- 4 spring onions, finely sliced
- 90g (3oz) cream cheese
- 1tbsp tequila (optional)
- 1 garlic clove
- Zest and juice of 1 lime
- 2 red chillies, finely sliced
- Fresh coriander leaves, to serve

1 Heat the air fryer to 180°C/350°F. Spray the tortillas with the oil, sprinkle over the sea salt. Cut into quarters and air fry in batches for 4 minutes.
2 For the guacamole, mash together the avocados, spring onions, cream cheese, tequila and garlic to a rough consistency. Stir in the lime zest and juice, and serve the guacamole topped with the chillies and coriander, alongside the tortilla chips.

Cook's Tip
Gochugang is a fermented red chilli paste that epitomises Korean flavours. You can find it in any Chinese or Japanese supermarket.

Korean Chicken Wings

The air fryer makes the best chicken wings ever – light, super-crispy with no greasiness.

Serves 8 • Ready in 1 hour

- 3tbsp plain flour
- 3tbsp potato or rice flour
- 2tbsp cornflour
- 1tsp baking powder
- 1.5kg (3lb 6oz) free-range chicken wings
- 2tsp toasted sesame seeds
- 1 bunch spring onions, finely sliced

For the sauce;

- 5 garlic cloves, crushed
- 4cm (1½in) piece ginger, grated
- 4tbsp gochujang paste (see Cook's Tip)
- 4tbsp rice wine vinegar
- 3tbsp light brown sugar
- 4tbsp maple syrup
- 1tbsp toasted sesame oil

1 For the sauce, put all the ingredients into a small pan. Place over a medium-high heat until beginning to bubble; reduce the heat and cook, stirring, for 10 mins, or until thickened and syrupy. Remove from the heat and set aside.

2 Mix together the flours, baking powder, 1tsp black pepper and 2tsp sea salt in a bowl. Add the chicken, toss to coat, then gently shake off any excess. Heat the air fryer to 200°C/400°F. Air fry the chicken in batches for 10 minutes, turning halfway through, then brush over the sauce and cook for 4 minutes.

3 Serve the sticky wings piled up with the sesame seeds and thinly sliced spring onions scattered over. Any leftover sauce can be re-heated and drizzled over the wings.

Cook's Tip

Gochugang is a fermented red chilli paste that epitomises Korean flavours. You can find it in any Chinese or Japanese supermarket.

Hortopitakia – salty cheese puffs

These little Greek pastries are normally fried, but they work brilliantly in an air fryer, without the fat and the faff!

Makes 8 • Ready in 45 minutes

- 100g (3½oz) Swiss chard
- ½ small bulb fennel
- 2 garlic cloves, finely chopped
- 3 spring onions
- 1 tsp olive oil
- 100g (3½oz) spinach
- 45g (1½oz) shredded kale
- 1tsp cumin powder
- 200g (7oz) crumbled feta
- 450g (1lb) puff pastry
- 1 egg beaten, to glaze

1 Roughly chop the chard, fennel, garlic and spring onions, and lightly fry in 1tsp olive oil until starting to soften. Add 2tbsp water to the hot pan, throw in the spinach and kale, and use the steam to wilt. Add the cumin. Season with pepper only for now, as adding feta later can be salty enough. Transfer to a bowl, drain the excess water, squeezing it out with your hands, and allow to cool before adding the feta.
2 Roll out the pastry to 3mm (0.1in) thickness and cut into 8 rounds (15-20cm/6-8in diameter). Brush the edge of each round with egg wash, put 1tbsp of filling on one side, fold over and crimp with a fork.
3 Brush the pastries with the beaten egg. Heat the air fryer to 200°C/400°F. Air fry, without turning, for 12 minutes, until beautifully puffed up and golden.

Halloumi fries

These are usually deep-fried, but cooked in an air fryer, the result is just as melting, crisp and delicious.

Makes 40 · Ready in 30 minutes

- **2 x 225g (8oz) blocks halloumi**
- **3tbsp plain flour**
- **1tbsp smoked paprika**
- **1tbsp chilli powder**
- **2 eggs, beaten**
- **120g (4oz) panko breadcrumbs**
- **Oil spray**
- **Dips to serve, such as sriracha mayonnaise**

Slice your blocks of halloumi into sticks, each one roughly the size of a thick finger. Combine the flour, paprika and chilli and place on a plate. Pour the egg into a shallow dish, and scatter the breadcrumbs onto a final plate. Coat the halloumi sticks with the flour mixture, then the egg and finally the panko. Heat the air fryer to 180°C/350°F. Spray the sticks with oil. Air fry the sticks in batches for 8 minutes, turning half way through.

"Baba ganoush is a great dip to serve alongside hummus and taramasalata"

Baba ganoush

This moreish Middle Eastern dip can be made in an air fryer in less than half the time of a conventional oven.

Serves 10 · Ready in 30 minutes

- **3 medium aubergines**
- **Olive oil spray**
- **2 garlic cloves**
- **2½tbsp tahini paste**
- **1tsp cumin seeds, toasted**
- **3tbsp lemon juice (approx 1 lemon)**
- **Handful of fresh parsley, chopped**
- **Pomegranate seeds (optional)**

1 Heat the air fryer to 200°C/400°F. Cut the aubergines in half lengthways, and score the flesh in a criss-cross pattern, being careful not to cut through the skin. Spray the aubergine halves with the oil, put into the air fryer skin side down (you may need to do this in 2 batches), and air fry for 20 minutes until the flesh is soft.

2 Remove from the oven and leave to cool. Place the garlic, tahini, cumin, remaining olive oil, aubergine flesh (discard the skins) and lemon juice into a food processor and blitz until it reaches a dip consistency. Season to taste and scatter with parsley and pomegranate seeds.

Tuna and pepper quesadillas

A simple, speedy lunch for two, which is light and healthy to serve with a green salad.

Serves 2 • Ready in 15 minutes

- 160g (5 ½oz) tin tuna, drained
- Juice of 1 lime
- 50g (2oz) sweetcorn, drained
- Handful of coriander, chopped
- 2tbsp chipotle sauce
- 2 roasted red peppers, drained from jar, chopped
- 3tbsp grated Cheddar
- 2 tortilla wraps
- Olive oil spray
- 1 avocado, quartered, stone removed
- 1 tomato, deseeded, diced
- 2 spring onions, sliced
- 100g (4oz) rocket

1 In a bowl, mix together the tuna, 1tsp lime juice, sweetcorn, coriander, chipotle sauce and peppers. Season well. If the peppers were in brine, rinse and dry them first.

2 Mash together the avocado, remaining lime juice and seasoning, then stir through most of the tomato and spring onion.

3 Put the tuna filling on one half of each tortilla. Sprinkle over the cheese, ensuring it's on the edge, as it makes the "glue" to stick the quesadillas together in the air fryer. Fold over the other side and push to seal. Heat the air fryer to 180°C/350°F. Spray with oil and cook for a minute, then use a fish slice to flatten it once the cheese has started to melt. Cook for a further 3 minutes, flip over, spray and cook for another 4 minutes.

4 Serve the hot quesadilla, cut into wedges, with the guacamole, salad and the remaining tomato, onion and coriander.

Asian sausage rolls

These have an added zing of spice and take just minutes to air fry.

Makes 22 • Ready in 35 minutes

- **400g (14oz) minced pork**
- **3tbsp kecap manis (sweet soy sauce)**
- **1tbsp sesame oil**
- **4 spring onions, finely sliced (including the green part)**
- **¼tsp Chinese five spice**
- **½tsp dried chilli flakes**
- **375g (13oz) puff pastry**
- **1 egg, beaten**
- **2tbsp sesame seeds**

1 Mix the mince with the kecap manis, sesame oil, spring onions, five spice and chilli flakes, and season well.
2 Roll out the pastry to 30x50cm (12x 19½in). Cut lengthwise in half. Spread the meat down each length, and brush one side with egg. Fold over the opposite side of the pastry and use a fork to seal. Trim the edge. Brush with egg and sprinkle over sesame seeds. Cut into 3cm-long (1.2in) rolls.
3 Heat the air fryer to 200°C/400°F. Bake in batches for 8 minutes. If baking from frozen, add 2-3 extra minutes to the cooking time, checking they are cooked through and piping hot before serving.

"It's worth making a few batches of these sausage rolls to have a stash in the freezer"

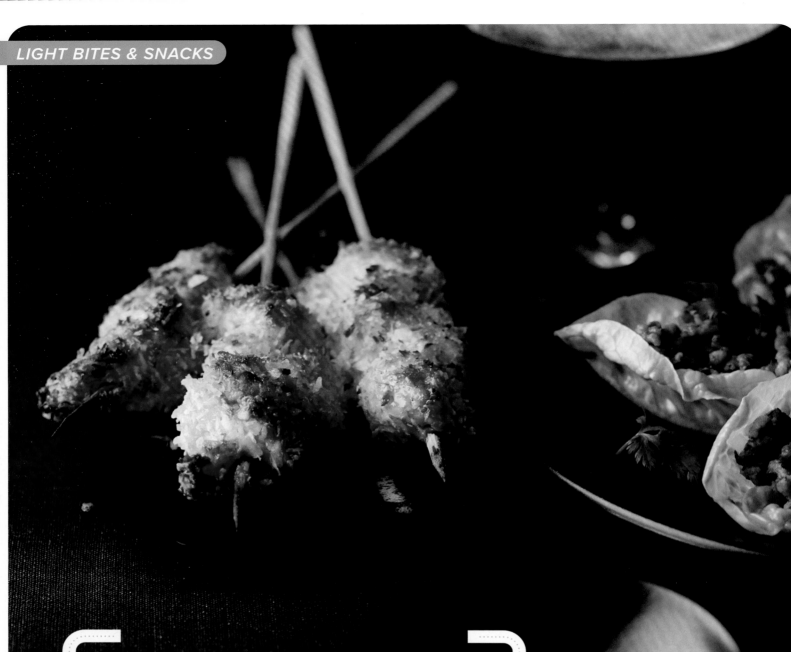

Coconut chicken skewers

If you have time, marinate these the day before for extra flavour and tender chicken.

Makes 12 • Ready in 25 minutes

- **2tbsp Thai red curry paste**
- **5tbsp coconut cream**
- **4 skinless chicken breasts, cut into thick strips**
- **100g (3½oz) desiccated coconut oil spray**
- **Sweet chilli sauce, to serve**
  You will need:
- **12 small skewers, which fit into your air fryer basket**

1 Mix the curry paste with the coconut cream. Season with salt and black pepper. Add the chicken and marinate in the fridge for 2-24 hours.
2 Thread the chicken onto the skewers.
3 Heat the air fryer to 200°C/400°F. Put the skewers on to a large plate, sprinkle the coconut all over, then air fry in 2 batches for 8 minutes.

Sriracha chicken spring rolls

Your air fryer takes away the need to deep-fry these mini spring rolls, but the result is just as light and crunchy.

Makes 18 • Ready in 40 minutes

- 150g (5oz) minced chicken breast
- 1 small carrot, julienned
- Handful of bean sprouts
- 3 spring onions, finely sliced
- Small bunch coriander, chopped
- 3tbsp sriracha sauce
- 250g (9oz) filo pastry
- Oil spray

To serve:
- Sriracha mayo
- Soy sauce

1 Mix together the chicken, vegetables, coriander and sriracha sauce. Season with sea salt and freshly ground black pepper.

2 Cut the filo pastry into 18 x 13cm (7 x 5 in) squares – it's easy with kitchen scissors. Cover with a damp cloth to prevent the pastry drying out as you work.

3 Take a square and lay it on your board with a point facing you. Spoon around 1tbsp of the chicken across the diamond. Bring the left and right point into the centre of the square, then bring the bottom point up to the centre, so you have an unclosed envelope shape. Roll this upwards, brushing the top point with a little water to seal the roll. Repeat with the remaining mixture and pastry. As each one is done, spray with oil and set aside.

4 Heat the air fryer to 190°C/375°F. Cook the rolls in batches for 10 minutes, turning each one half way through. Serve on a platter with your favourite dipping sauces.

Falafels with green goddess dressing

Serve these crisp little chickpea fritters with a crunchy salad for a healthy lunch.

Makes 16 • Ready in 35 minutes

- 2 x 400g (14oz) tins chickpeas, drained and rinsed
- 1 small onion, finely chopped
- 1 garlic clove, crushed
- 2tbsp coriander, chopped
- 1tbsp parsley, chopped, plus extra leaves to garnish
- ¼tsp cayenne pepper
- 2tsp garam masala
- 1tsp baking powder
- 1½tbsp plain flour
- Sesame seeds, to coat
- Olive oil spray

For the dressing:
- 200ml (7fl oz) mayonnaise
- 1tsp capers, rinsed and finely chopped
- 4 good-quality anchovies, from a tin, finely chopped, or 2tsp anchovy paste
- 1 small bunch chives, roughly chopped
- 1 small bunch parsley, roughly chopped
- A few sprigs of tarragon, leaves only, roughly chopped
- 1 garlic clove, crushed
- 3tbsp crème fraîche or soured cream
- Tabasco and lemon juice, to serve

1 Mix the chickpeas with the onion, garlic, coriander and parsley. Put a third of the mixture into a food processor and pulse until it's finely chopped and starts to hold itself together, then transfer to a bowl. Don't over-blend as it will become gluey. Repeat for the remainder of the chickpea mixture.
2 Add the spices, baking powder and flour, and season well. Use your hands to mix, then cover and chill for at least 1hr, or until ready to shape.
3 To make the dressing, blitz all the ingredients in a food processor until mostly broken up and a bright green colour. Season if necessary. Set aside.
4 With slightly wet hands, shape a heaped tbsp of the falafel mixture into a small patty, then roll in sesame seeds and put on a baking tray. Repeat until you have 16 falafels. Spray with olive oil.
5 Heat the air fryer to 180°C/350°F. Air fry the falafels in 2 batches for 11 minutes. Arrange on a platter with the dressing.

"Falafels make a great party nibble, or serve as a light lunch with a crisp green salad"

Cook's Tip
Replace the plain flour with chickpea (gram) flour or gluten-free flour for any gluten-free guests.

Cook's Tip

When air frying these pastries, don't use a silicone or other liners, or the centre will be a little soggy.

Puffed garlic mushroom tartlets

You can assemble these veggie tartlets in advance, then pop them in the air fryer when you are ready to serve.

Makes 6 • Ready in 25 minutes

- 250g (9oz) chestnut mushrooms, sliced
- 3 garlic cloves, crushed
- Olive oil spray
- 2tsp thyme leaves, plus extra to serve
- 325g (11oz) ready-rolled puff pastry
- 150g (5oz) garlic and herb flavoured cream cheese
- 1 egg, lightly beaten
- 1tbsp hazelnuts, roasted and chopped

1 Heat the air fryer to 200°C/400°F. Mix the mushrooms and garlic together, give them a good spray of oil. Put them into a dish which fits the air fryer basket, then air fry for 8 minutes, stirring halfway through. Set aside,

2 Cut the pastry into 6 squares, scoring a 2cm (¾in) border around the edge. Divide the cheese between them and top with the mushrooms. Brush the pastry border with the egg. Air fry in batches for 8 minutes, until puffed and golden. Top with the extra thyme leaves and hazelnuts.

Goat's cheese & fig stars

Lightly melted cheese with sweet figs and honey ready in minutes.

Makes 20 • Ready in 20 minutes

- 325g (11oz) all butter ready- rolled puff pastry
- 1 egg, beaten
- 1 small log goat's cheese, cut into 20 half-moon shapes
- 4 figs, each one cut into 5 wedges
- A generous drizzle of honey
- ½tsp sumac

You will need:
- Star biscuit cutter

1 Heat the air fryer to 190°C/375°F. Cut out star shapes from the sheet of puff pastry and place on a baking tray. Brush each shape with egg wash. Top with a piece of goat's cheese and a fig wedge.

2 Air fry in batches for 5 minutes on a silicon or parchment mat. Drizzle with honey and sprinkle over the sumac. Allow to cool slightly before serving.

"Try making these mini pastries with Brie or Camembert"

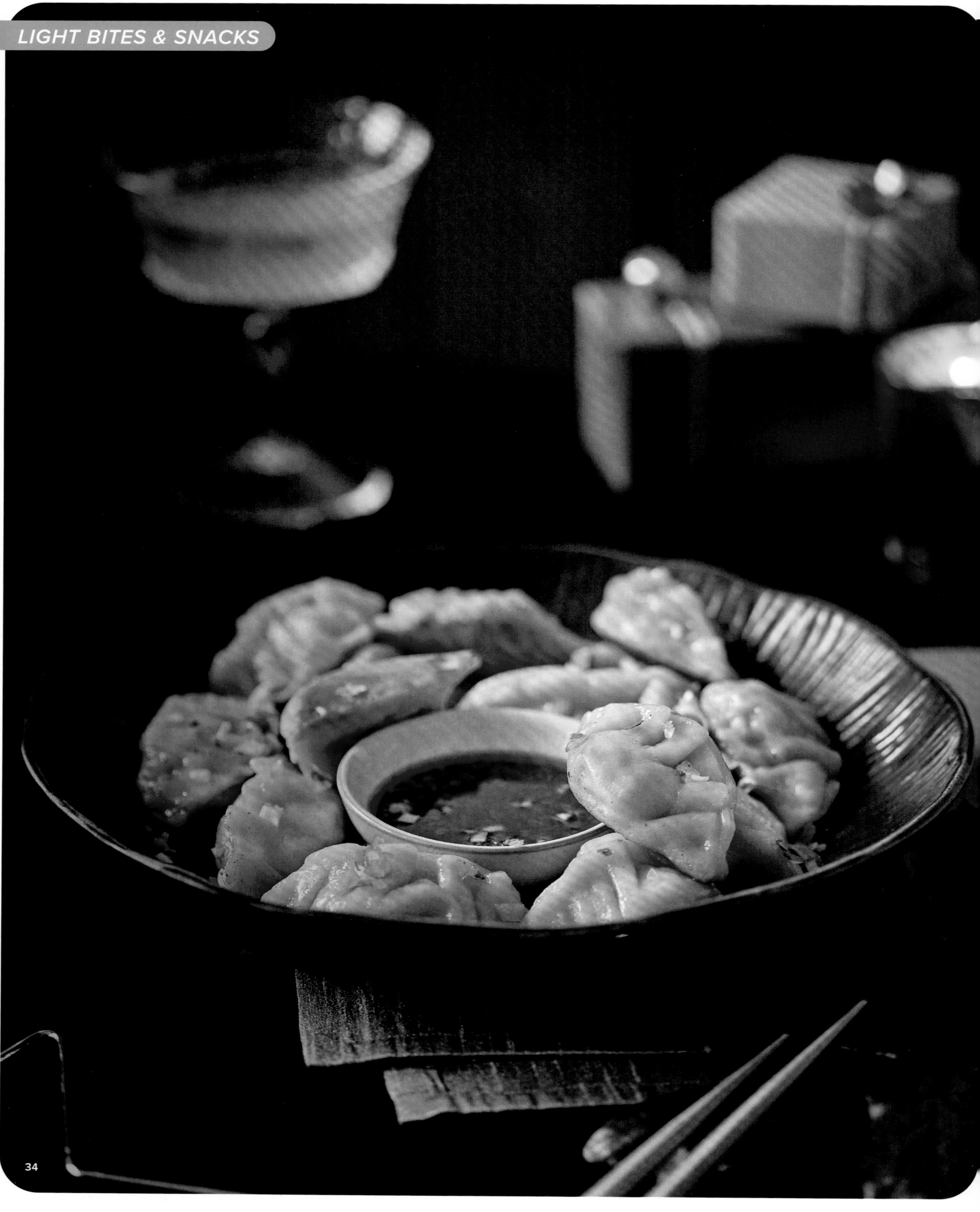

Chicken, sprout and spring onion gyoza

Make a batch for the freezer for a great snack or nibble with drinks. Best of all, you can cook them from frozen. If you're pushed for time, buy the wrappers from Asian supermarkets.

Makes around 30 · Ready in 20 minutes

200g (7oz) plain flour, sifted
Oil spray
For the filling:
- 125g (4oz) chicken breast, cut into chunks
- 3 spring onions, sliced
- 60g (2oz) Brussels sprouts, sliced
- 2tsp grated ginger
- 2tsp grated garlic
- 3tsp soy sauce
- 2tsp toasted sesame seed oil, plus extra, to drizzle
You will need:
- A 10cm (4in) round cutter

1 Mix the flour and ¼tsp fine salt in a large bowl. Pour in 150ml (5fl oz) hand-hot water, a little at a time, and mix until combined. You may not need all the water. Transfer to a lightly dusted work surface and knead for 10 mins until smooth and elastic. Divide the dough into 2 and roll into balls. Wrap in cling film and rest for 30 mins.
2 For the filling, blitz all the ingredients in a food processor. Fry 1tsp of the mix to check the seasoning; adjust if necessary.
3 Lightly dust a work surface and a baking tray. Roll out the dough until as thin as possible. Cut out circles with the cutter, transfer to the tray and cover loosely with cling film to prevent them from drying. You should have around 30 gyoza wrappers.
4 Spoon 1tsp of filling into the centre of each wrapper, wet the rim

with water then crimp together using your thumb and forefinger. You can cook them straight away or cover with cling film and refrigerate for up to 6 hrs. If freezing, place the baking tray in the freezer – once the gyoza are solid, you can transfer to a freezer bag for easy storage.
5 To cook from frozen, spray the gyoza thoroughly with oil, add a little water to the air fryer underneath the basket. Heat the air fryer to 180°C/350°F. Air fry in batches, ensuring they aren't too close together, for 6 minutes, turning halfway through. To cook from fresh, allow 4-5 minutes.
6 Ensure the gyoza are piping hot and serve with a dipping sauce. We like a mix of chilli oil, soy, sesame oil and lime juice.

Cheesy olive bites

Perfect to serve with drinks, these take a bit of effort to prepare, but are air fried in minutes.

Makes 50 · Ready in 1 hour

- 100g (3½oz) unsalted butter, softened
- 100g (3½oz) Cheddar cheese, finely grated
- 150g (5oz) plain flour
- ¼tsp cayenne pepper
- 1 egg, beaten
- 3 dashes Worcestershire sauce
- 50 (about 150g/5oz) pimento stuffed olives (pitted)
- Oil spray

1 Beat the butter until creamy in a large mixing bowl, add the cheese and mix well. Stir in the flour, cayenne pepper and a pinch of sea salt.
2 Beat the egg with 2tbsp cold water and the Worcestershire sauce. Add to the dough and mix just until incorporated. Refrigerate for 30 mins.
3 Remove the olives from the jar and dry with kitchen paper. Tear off an olive-sized piece of dough, press into a disc, place an olive onto the disc and shape the dough around it, pinching to repair breaks. Place onto a baking tray. Repeat the process with the remaining dough and olives.
4 Heat the air fryer to 200°C/400°F. Spray the bites with oil, then air fry in 3 batches for 8 minutes, giving them a shake in the basket after 5 minutes.

Ham and Manchego croquettes

These are utterly moreish – prepare ahead and put back into the air fryer to reheat.

Makes 20-24 • Ready in 40 minutes, plus chilling

- 4tbsp olive oil
- 1 shallot, finely chopped
- 75g (1½in) Ibérico ham, diced very small, plus 75g (1½in) to serve
- 100g (3½oz) plain flour
- 75ml (5tbsp) vegetable stock
- 300ml (10 fl oz) milk
- 50g (3tbsp) Manchego cheese, grated

For the crumb:
- 75g (5tbsp) plain flour
- 2 large eggs, beaten
- 100g (3½oz) breadcrumbs (we like panko crumbs, which are widely available)
- Oil spray
- Quince paste, to serve

1 Heat the oil in a pan, add the shallot and sauté until soft but not coloured. Stir in the diced ham, fry for 1 minute, then add the flour and fry over a medium heat until the mixture is golden.
2 Heat the stock and milk in a small pan until hot but not boiling. Then gradually add this liquid to the roux, stirring all the time. Continue to cook for 5 minutes until it thickens. Add the cheese and season with black pepper. Pour the sauce onto a small baking tray then cover with clingfilm. Leave it to cool then put it in the fridge for 1 hr.
3 For the crumb, put the flour, eggs and crumbs into 3 bowls. Dust your hands with flour, take some of the cheese mixture and roll it to a walnut-sized ball. Dust with flour, then roll in the egg and then the breadcrumbs. Put on a tray and chill for 30-45 mins.
4 Heat the air fryer to 200°C/400°F. Spray the croquettes with oil, then cook in batches for 6 minutes. Serve with the quince paste and slices of ham.

*p*64
Easy speedy
pizza recipes to
feed the kids!

MAIN MEALS

Spicy paneer kebabs

Paneer is a soft, mild, non-melting cheese, widely used across the Indian Continent. It holds its shape well, so is great for the air fryer.

Serves 2 • Ready in 10 minutes, plus marinating

- 200g (7oz) paneer
- 1tbsp coriander seeds
- 1tsp each cumin and turmeric
- 2tbsp sunflower oil
- 1tsp sea salt
- Juice of 2 limes
- 2 red onions, cut into chunks
  To serve:
- Lime wedges
- 1 cucumber, peeled into ribbons

1 Cut the paneer into 12 chunks. Put into a bowl. Toast the coriander seeds in a dry frying pan then crush with a mortar and pestle. Mix the coriander in a separate bowl with cumin, turmeric, oil, salt and lime juice. Mix this well with the paneer, cover and leave to marinate for a few hours or overnight.
2 Heat the air fryer to 200°C/400°F. Thread the paneer onto 4 skewers, using 3 chunks per skewer, separating each piece with a chunk of red onion. Air fry for 5 minutes, turning halfway through. Serve with lime wedges and cucumber.

"Soft in the centre, yet crisp on the outside, paneer makes a perfect veggie meal"

Stuffed peppers with harissa yoghurt

Harissa is a spicy chilli paste from North Africa. Paired with thick yoghurt, it makes a great side or dip.

Serves 6 • Ready in 1 hour

For the peppers:
- 1 onion, chopped
- 1tbsp olive oil
- 2 cloves garlic, finely chopped
- ½tsp ground cinnamon
- 1tsp ground cumin
- 200g (7oz) puy or green lentils, rinsed
- 350ml (12fl oz) vegetable stock
- 150g (5oz) spinach leaves
- 2tbsp raisins
- 2tbsp pine nuts, toasted in a dry pan
- 2tbsp chopped mint
- 2tbsp chopped parsley
- 6 red peppers, halved and deseeded
  For the yoghurt:
- 2tbsp harissa paste
- 300g (10oz) thick yoghurt

1 Gently soften the onion in the oil for 10 mins. Add the garlic, cinnamon and cumin and cook for 1 min. Stir in the lentils and stock. Bring to the boil, then simmer for 15 mins until the lentils are tender, but still hold their shape. Heat the air fryer to 200°C/400°F.
2 Fold in the spinach just before removing from the heat, letting it wilt. Stir in the raisins, pine nuts, mint and parsley, and season to taste.
3 Lay the peppers out, cut sides up, and fill with the lentil mixture. Pair up the halves and tie together with string. Wrap the peppers tightly in oiled foil. Air fry for 15 minutes, in two batches if you need to. The peppers will keep hot wrapped in the foil. Swirl the harissa into the yoghurt and serve with the peppers.

Cheese and tomato quesadilla

You will probably need to cook the tortillas one at a time in an air fryer, but they are so quick to cook, they will remain hot, melting and utterly delicious.

Serves 2 • Ready in 20 mins

- 150g (5oz) Jarlsberg or Gruyère cheese, grated
- 50g (2oz) Cheddar, grated
- 50g (2oz) cherry tomatoes, quartered
- Small handful coriander, leaves picked
- 4 flour tortillas
- Few drops of Tabasco sauce
- Oil spray

1 Divide the cheese, tomatoes and coriander leaves between 2 tortillas, ensuring some of the cheese is right at the edge. Season well with Tabasco, salt and pepper, then top with the remaining tortillas to form a sandwich. Press down firmly on each one to flatten.

2 Heat the air fryer to 180°C/350°F. Spray with oil and cook the first quesadilla for a minute, then use a fish slice to flatten it once the cheese has started to melt. Cook for a further 3 minutes, flip over, spray and cook for another 4 minutes. Cut into wedges and serve immediately with a selection of dips.

"Try serving these moreish quesadillas with guacamole, sriracha mayonnaise and a spicy tomato salsa"

Cook's Tip
You can microwave the potatoes and prepare the sauce, then cook the potatoes in the air fryer just before serving.

Spanish-style beans on jacket potato

It doesn't take much less time to air fry the perfect jacket potato than using the oven, but if it's just for one or two potatoes, it's more energy-efficient. Microwaving them first saves time.

Serves 2 • Ready in 30 minutes

- 2 large potatoes, scrubbed
- 1tsp oil
- 1 small red onion, diced
- 1 red pepper, diced
- 1 garlic clove, crushed
- 1tsp smoked paprika
- 400g (14oz) tin cannellini beans, drained and rinsed
- 150ml (5fl oz) tomato passata
- Pinch of sugar
- Oil spray
- 2tbsp crème fraîche
- Small handful parsley, chopped

1 Pierce the potatoes with a fork and microwave them for 8-10 mins until just tender.
2 Meanwhile, heat the oil in a pan, add the onion and pepper and cook for 5 mins. Stir in the garlic and paprika and cook for a few mins to soften. Add the beans, passata, a splash of water and sugar. Warm through for 5 mins.
3 Heat the air fryer to 200°C/400°F. Spray the potatoes with oil, grind over some sea salt and air fry for 10 minutes until crisp.
4 Split the jacket potatoes, spoon in the beans, and top with the crème fraîche and parsley to serve.

Miso aubergine with grain salad

A staple in Japanese cuisine, miso offers an umami or savoury flavour to this vegan dish. If your vegans don't eat honey, replace with maple syrup.

Serves 4 • Ready in 35 minutes

- 2 large aubergines, halved
- 2tbsp miso paste
- 1tbsp honey
- 1tbsp sesame oil
- 1tbsp soy sauce
- 1 garlic clove, crushed

For the salad:
- 2 x 250g (9oz) packs mixed, cooked grains
- 200g (7oz) frozen edamame beans
- ½ a bunch coriander, plus extra to serve

For the dressing:
- 2tbsp soy sauce
- 2tsp sesame oil
- 2tsp honey
- Juice of 2 limes

To serve:
- 4 spring onions, sliced
- 1 red chilli, finely sliced

1 Heat the air fryer to 180°C/350°F. Score the aubergines in a diagonal checkerboard style. Combine the miso, honey, sesame oil, soy sauce and garlic, and brush over the aubergine halves – you won't use all of it, but reserve the rest for later. Air fry for 15 minutes, then re-glaze with the remaining miso mixture and air fry for a further 10 minutes.

2 Meanwhile, microwave the grains for 2 mins on high and cook the edamame for 5 mins in a pan of simmering water. When cooked, combine the grains and edamame in a bowl. Stir through the coriander.

3 Mix together dressing ingredients and stir through; season well to taste. To serve, divide the salad between 4 plates and top each with an aubergine half, plus spring onions, coriander and chilli.

Cheese soufflé

A perfectly glamorous lunch for one, made even easier with an air fryer.

Serves 1 • Ready in 15 mins

- **1tbsp butter, plus a little extra for greasing**
- **1tbsp plain flour**
- **5tbsp milk**
- **1 egg, separated**
- **30g (1oz) mature Cheddar, grated**
- **1tsp dried English mustard powder or Dijon mustard**
- **1tbsp Parmesan, grated**
- **A few slices of red onion (optional)**
  You will need:
- **1 large ramekin or similar ovenproof dish, approx 10cm (4in) diameter and 6cm (2 ½in) deep.**

1 Heat the butter in a small saucepan and add the flour and mustard powder. Slowly stir in the milk, stirring constantly, until the mixture has thickened. Remove from the heat and add the egg yolk, grated Cheddar and Dijon mustard, if using. Heat the air fryer to 190°C/375°F.

2 Grease a ramekin with a little butter and dust with the grated Parmesan. Whisk the egg white until doubled in size and frothy. Once the cheese mixture has cooled slightly, gently fold in the egg white with a balloon whisk.

3 Pour the mixture into the ramekin, top with sliced red onion and air fry for 11 minutes until risen and golden brown. Eat warm with a green salad.

"Soufflés are much easier to make than you may think"

Black bean quesadillas with salsa

The trick to making quesadillas in an air fryer is to ensure there's cheese around the edge. This will act as the "glue" to hold the tortillas together – otherwise the power of the fan will blow them open.

Serves 2 • Ready in 20 minutes

- **400g (14oz) tin black beans, drained**
- **50g (2oz) tinned sweetcorn, drained**
- **¼tsp chilli flakes**
- **1tsp smoked paprika**
- **3 spring onions, thinly sliced**
- **150g (5oz) Wensleydale or any strong cheese, grated**
- **Small bunch coriander, finely chopped**
- **Oil spray**
- **2 flour tortillas**
- **Salsa and lime wedges, to serve**

1 Mix together the black beans, sweetcorn, chilli flakes, smoked paprika, spring onions and half the cheese and coriander, then season.
2 Sprinkle a quarter of the cheese over half of one tortilla and top with half the bean mixture. Top with another handful of cheese, ensuring you have cheese on the border, and fold the tortilla over. Repeat with the other tortilla.
3 Heat the air fryer to 180°C/350°F. Spray with oil and cook for a minute, then use a fish slice to flatten it once the cheese has started to melt. Cook for a further 3 minutes, flip over, spray and cook for another 4 minutes.
4 Halve each quesadilla and serve with salsa and the remaining coriander, and lime wedges on the side.

Pea & potato cakes

Peas, potatoes and halloumi — what isn't to love?

Serves 4 (makes 8) • Ready in 30 minutes

- **750g (1½lb) sweet potatoes**
- **75g (2½oz) frozen petits pois (baby peas), thawed**
- **100g (3½oz) halloumi cheese, diced**
- **Zest and juice of a lime**
- **5tbsp polenta (fine cornmeal)**
- **Oil spray**
- **Salad and sweet chilli sauce, to serve**

1 Prick the sweet potatoes all over with a fork and microwave for 10min, until cooked through. Remove from the microwave and carefully slice in half to cool.
2 Scoop the sweet potato flesh into a large bowl. Stir through the peas, diced halloumi, lime zest, 3tbsp polenta and season well. Shape into eight patties and dust with the remaining polenta.
3 Heat the air fryer to 180°C/350°F. Spray the potato cakes with oil. Air fry for 8 minutes on a silicone or parchment liner, turning halfway through and spraying again. If you need to air fry in two batches, simply return the first batch to the air fryer to heat through for 2 minutes. Serve with a squeeze of lime, salad and sweet chilli sauce.

> "Halloumi holds its shape when cooked, but still softens to perfection"

Bangladeshi aubergine & courgette curry

A flavoursome vegan dish, which even die-hard meat eaters will love!

Serves 4 • Ready in 40 minutes

- **2 aubergines**
- **200g (7oz) baby courgettes**
- **4tbsp vegetable oil**
- **2tbsp freshly grated root ginger**
- **2 garlic cloves, peeled and grated**
- **1-2 green large chillies, finely sliced**
- **2tsp fennel seeds**
- **1tsp cumin seeds**
- **1tbsp roughly ground coriander seeds**
- **½tsp ground turmeric**
- **400g (14oz) tin chopped tomatoes**
- **A good handful each of fresh chopped coriander and mint**
- **Rice or naan bread, to serve**

1 Cut the aubergines in half and then cut them in half lengthways into 6 or 8 wedges. Halve the baby courgettes. Toss all the veg with a little salt and set aside in a colander for 20 mins. Heat the air fryer to 180°C/350°F.
2 Quickly rinse and dry the aubergines and courgettes. Toss them in 2tbsp of the oil and season well. Air fry for 8-10 minutes (you may need to do this in 2 batches) until well browned. Shake the drawer half way through cooking.
3 Meanwhile, mix the ginger, garlic and chilli in a mortar with 3tbsp water and grind to paste with a pestle, or mix in a small bowl.
4 Put the remaining oil (2tbsp) in a frying pan, and add the fennel and cumin seeds. When they start to sizzle, add the ginger paste and fry for another few mins. Add the coriander seeds and turmeric, fry for 1 min, then add the tomatoes and season generously with salt and black pepper. Cover and leave to simmer for 8-10 mins until reduced and thickened slightly. Add a little water if it gets too thick. Stir in the fresh herbs.
5 Divide the vegetables between 4 warm dishes and spoon the hot sauce over. Serve with rice or naan bread.

Pitta pizzas with avocado and Brie

Camembert would work well in this quick recipe, or Cambozola goes down well with blue cheese lovers.

Serves 2 • Ready in 10 minutes

- **3tbsp tomato passata (see Cook's Tip)**
- **2 pitta breads**
- **Oil spray**
- **125g (4oz) ripe Brie, cut into long, thin slices**
- **Large handful seedless green grapes, halved**
- **1 avocado, peeled and chopped**
- **Handful parsley leaves, roughly chopped**

1 Heat the air fryer to 200°C/400°F. Spray the pitta breads, then air fry for 2 minutes, flipping half way through and spraying again. Remove from the air fryer.
2 Spread the passata evenly over the pittas and top with 3 to 4 slices of Brie. Air fry for 3-4 minutes, until the Brie is melted and bubbling.
3 Remove from the oven and top with the grapes, avocado and parsley. Serve immediately.

Pitta pizzas

Using pitta breads as a "pizza" base makes a speedy meal for two. Mix and match the toppings as you prefer.

Serves 2 • Ready in 10 minutes

- **2 wholemeal pitta breads**
- **Oil spray**
- **3tbsp tomato passata (see Cook's Tip)**
- **½ red onion, thinly sliced**
- **60g (2½ oz) mozzarella cheese, thinly sliced handful of olives, sliced**
- **2tsp pesto (make sure it's vegetarian if serving to vegetarians)**
- **6 pitted green olives, sliced**
- **A handful of rocket leaves**

1 Heat the air fryer to 200°C/400°F. Spray the pitta breads, then air fry for 2 minutes, flipping half way through and spraying again. Remove.
2 Spread the passata evenly over the pittas and top with the mozzarella. Air fry for 3-4 minutes, until the cheese is melted and bubbling.
3 Remove from the air fryer and top with the pesto, olives, red pepper and rocket. Serve immediately.

Cook's Tip

If you have a good Turkish or Middle Eastern deli nearby, look out for red pepper paste, known in Turkish as "biter salcasi". Slightly spicy with a good texture, it makes a great base for these pizzas, but added to dips, pasta sauces and salad dressings, it adds masses of flavour and you'll find plenty of uses for it.

Curried leftover veggie pasties

Curried potatoes and root veg work a treat with spices. The pastry is worth the extra effort, but swap for shop-bought shortcrust if you prefer.

Serves 4 • Ready in 1 hour

For the pastry:
- **300g (10oz) plain flour, plus extra to dust**
- **200g (7oz) cold unsalted butter, cubed**
- **2tbsp nigella (kalonji) seeds**
- **1 medium egg, lightly beaten**
- **3-4tbsp milk**
- **2tsp white wine vinegar**
- **1 egg, beaten, to glaze**

For the filling:
- **400g (14oz) leftover roasted veg, cut into 2cm (¾in) chunks, we used potatoes, carrots and parsnips**
- **200g (7oz) spinach leaves, blanched**
- **1tsp coriander seeds, toasted and ground**
- **1tsp fennel seeds, toasted and ground**
- **1tsp ground cumin**
- **2tbsp lime pickle**
- **Handful coriander, roughly chopped**
- **Juice 1 lime**

1 Put the flour and 1tsp salt in a mixing bowl. Rub in the cubed butter until the mixture resembles breadcrumbs. Stir in the nigella seeds and mix through. Add the egg, milk and vinegar, and combine using a table knife. Using your hands, work the mixture until it comes together to form a dough; it should be soft but not sticky. Shape the dough into a ball, flatten into a disc, cover in cling film and chill.

2 In a large bowl, combine all the filling ingredients.

3 Divide the pastry into 4 equal bits. Roll out one piece on a lightly floured surface to form a circle roughly 4-5mm (0.1-0.2in) thick.

4 Pile a quarter of the filling onto one half of the pastry, leaving a 2.5cm (1in) border around the edge. Brush the edges with a little beaten egg, then fold the other half over and press to enclose the filling. Crimp the edges of the pastry with a fork, and place on a large plate.

5 Repeat with the remaining pastry and filling. Brush the pasties with the egg wash, chill for 20 mins then egg wash again. Heat the air fryer to 180°C/350°F.

6 Bake for 10 minutes, flip over, brush with egg and air fry for a further 10 minutes until golden. Serve with the fresh chutney or raita.

Chickpea and butternut squash burgers with carrot slaw

If you are after a healthy veggie burger, then look no further.

Serves 4 • Ready in 40 mins plus chilling time

- 450g (1lb) butternut squash, peeled, de-seeded and sliced
- 400g (14oz) tin chickpeas, drained and rinsed
- 100g (3½oz) breadcrumbs
- 2tsp ground cumin
- 1tbsp ground coriander
- 1 egg, lightly beaten
- 4tbsp plain flour
- 2tbsp sesame seeds
- Oil spray
  To serve:
- ¼ of a red cabbage, shredded
- 2 carrots, shredded
- 1 cucumber, shredded
- Juice of 1 orange
- 4 multi-grain rolls
- 200g (7oz) hummus
- 60g (2oz) baby kale

1 Boil the butternut squash in a pan of salted water for 8 mins or until tender. Drain, taking care to remove all excess moisture.
2 Put the chickpeas and squash into a food processor and blend to finely chop. Season generously, add the breadcrumbs, cumin, coriander, egg and flour. Blend again to combine.
3 Divide the mixture into 4 and shape into 4 burger rounds, using a large, plain round cutter, to help you get a good shape. Pour the sesame seeds into a shallow dish. Press the veggie burgers into the sesame seeds and turn to coat evenly. Put on to a baking parchment-lined tray, cover and chill for 30 mins to firm up.
4 Heat the air fryer to 190°C/375°F. Spray the burgers with oil, then air fry for 12 minutes, turning halfway through cooking.
5 Combine the red cabbage, carrots, cucumber and orange juice together.
6 Lightly toast the buns, spread the base of each one with hummus, top with the burgers, a handful of carrot slaw and a few baby kale leaves.

Turkey & chorizo burgers

Air-fried burgers are always juicy, with little risk of them drying out. The addition of chorizo sausage adds a welcome kick of spice.

Serves 4 · Ready in 25 minutes

- **125g (4oz) diced raw chorizo sausage**
- **450g (1lb) minced turkey leg (or use chicken thighs, if you prefer)**
- **1 egg, beaten**
- **1tsp smoked paprika**
- **Oil spray**
- **4 slices of strong cheese**

1 Heat the air fryer to 190°C/375°F. Combine the chorizo, turkey mince, egg and paprika in a large bowl. Season well, and mix until blended. Shape the mixture into 4 burgers.
2 Spray the top of each burger and air fry for 15 minutes or so. (This will depend on the thickness of your burgers). Flip halfway through, spray again. Once the air fryer has stopped, top each burger with a slice of cheese and return to the air fryer for a minute. The reason for this is the fan will blow off the cheese! So ensure it's off, though the air fryer will still be hot.
3 Serve on toasted burger buns with pickles, slices of tomato and baby gem lettuce.

"Why not try to experiment with beef and veggie burgers in your air fryer too?"

Pork chops with orzo

A dish full of Mediterranean sunshine. If you can't find orzo, which is a small pasta shaped like a grain of rice, use macaroni and cook for a little longer.

Serves 4 • Ready in 30 minutes

- 4 x 250g (9oz) pork chops
- 6 fresh oregano sprigs
- 2 tbsp olive oil
- 3 medium onions, finely chopped (or use frozen)
- 1 red pepper, deseeded and finely chopped
- 3tbsp sun-dried tomato paste
- 200g (7oz) orzo pasta
- 20g (¾oz) parsley, leaves only, chopped
- 1 lemon, cut into 8 wedges, to serve

1 Heat the air fryer to 180°C/350°F. Rub 1tbsp oil into the chops or spray, season well, add the oregano sprigs and air fry for 12 minutes, turning once. Once fully cooked through, allow to rest.

2 Meanwhile, heat the remaining oil in a non-stick frying pan and gently cook the onions and pepper for 10 mins. Stir in the tomato paste and 150ml (5fl oz) water; simmer for 5 mins.

3 Cook the orzo according to the pack instructions. Drain, then toss with the vegetable sauce. Season with salt and black pepper then stir in the chopped parsley.

4 Spoon the orzo between 4 plates, top with the chops, with lemon wedges on the side.

Pork belly banh mi

A Vietnamese-inspired main meal sandwich, where the pork cooks so much quicker in an air fryer and saves heating the oven for a small quantity.

Serves 4 • Ready in 30 minutes plus marinating

- **4 thick slices pork belly**
- **Oil spray**
  For the pickled veg:
- **100ml (3½fl oz) rice wine vinegar**
- **2tsp caster sugar**
- **½tsp salt**
- **2tsp ginger, grated**
- **1 carrot, sliced thinly**
- **½ cucumber, peeled into ribbons**
  For the sandwich:
- **100ml (3½fl oz) soy sauce**
- **100ml (3½fl oz) sweet chilli sauce**
- **1 garlic clove, crushed**
- **1 long baguette, cut into 4**
  To serve:
- **Mayonnaise**
- **Shredded lettuce**
- **Bunch each coriander and Thai basil**
- **Zest and juice of 2 limes**
- **1 red or green chilli, finely sliced**

1 Heat the air fryer to 200°C/400F. Spray the pork slices and air fry for 8 minutes. Turn over the pork, spray again. Reduce the heat to 160°C/300°F and cook for a further 13 minutes. Put the pork into a small dish which will fit into your air fryer. Turn the air fryer back up to 180°C/350°F.
2 Meanwhile, make the pickle. Combine the rice wine vinegar, caster sugar, salt, ginger, carrot and cucumber in a bowl. Leave to stand for 30 mins to marinate.
3 In a bowl, mix together the soy sauce, sweet chilli sauce and garlic. Pour this over the belly slices and return to the air fryer for 2 mins. Allow to cool slightly before cutting into 2cm (0.8in) chunks.
4 Slice the baguette lengthways, spread with mayonnaise and add the lettuce and half the herbs. Top with the meat (whole pieces or slices), pickled veg, lime zest and juice, then scatter the remaining herbs and chilli over to serve.

Firecracker wings with dipping sauce

You can make these as hot — or not — as you like. Perfect served with a crunchy green salad.

Serves 3 • Ready in 40 minutes plus marinating overnight

For the marinade:
- 400ml (14fl oz) apple juice
- 80g (3oz) granulated sugar
- 180ml (6fl oz) white wine vinegar
- 2tsp chilli flakes
- 60g (2oz) salt
- 1tsp crushed black pepper
- 1.5kg (3lb) chicken wings

For the hot sauce:
- 100ml (3½fl oz) ketchup
- 4tbsp honey
- 5tbsp white wine vinegar
- 1tbsp mustard
- 1tbsp Worcestershire sauce
- 1tbsp soy sauce
- 4-6tbsp sriracha hot sauce
- 1tsp chilli powder

For the dipping sauce:
- 150ml (5fl oz) soured cream
- 3tbsp mayonnaise
- 50g (2oz) blue cheese, crumbled
- Juice of 1 large lemon

1 For the marinade, heat apple juice in a saucepan, then add the sugar, vinegar, chilli flakes, salt and black pepper. remove from the heat and add 1ltr (1¾pt) water. Place in a large, non-metallic container, and add the chicken wings. Stir well and leave in the fridge overnight to marinate.

2 Heat the air fryer to 200°F/400°F. Remove wings and discard marinade. Air fry the chicken in batches for 10 minutes.

3 Meanwhile, prepare the hot sauce by mixing together all the hot sauce ingredients. Brush the wings with the hot sauce and air fry for 4 minutes.

4 For the dipping sauce, mix together all the ingredients and season well to taste. Once ready, arrange the chicken wings on a platter and serve with the sauce on the side.

Chicken Kyiv

No frying required! This classic is easier than you think — it just needs a little time for chilling. Save time and buy pre-made garlic butter, too.

Serves 4 • Ready in 30 minutes plus chilling

- **4 boneless, skinless chicken breasts**
- **100g (3½oz) salted butter, softened**
- **2tbsp freshly chopped parsley**
- **3 garlic cloves, crushed**
- **2tbsp plain flour, well seasoned**
- **2 large eggs, beaten**
- **125g (4oz) panko breadcrumbs**

1 Use a sharp knife to slice the chicken part of the way through and open them out. Put each breast between 2 pieces of clingfilm and pound them to about 5mm (¼in) with a rolling pin — but carefully, as you don't want to tear the flesh.

2 Mix the butter, parsley, garlic and 1tsp freshly ground black pepper together. Divide the mixture into 4 portions and add into the centre of each piece of chicken. Fold up the chicken, tucking in the ends to make a parcel, and wrap in clingfilm. Chill for at least 30 mins.

3 Remove the clingfilm and coat the chicken in the seasoned flour. Then dip in the beaten egg and roll the chicken in the breadcrumbs. Chill for a further 30 mins.

4 Remove the chicken from the fridge and coat in the egg and breadcrumbs once more. Heat the air fryer to 180°C/350°F. Air fry for 12-15 minutes (depending on the size of the chicken breasts) until fully cooked through. Serve with greens and new potatoes.

67

Hunter's chicken

An air fryer makes this a super-speedy and tasty supper, the bacon keeping the chicken succulent and tender.

Serves 4 • Ready in 30 minutes

- **12 slices of pancetta or smoked streaky bacon**
- **4 boneless, skinless chicken breasts**
- **Oil spray**
- **150g (5oz) grated Gouda or Cheddar cheese**
  For the barbecue sauce:
- **90g (3oz) tomato ketchup**
- **1 garlic clove, crushed**
- **½tbsp white wine vinegar**
- **½tbsp sweet paprika**
- **Pinch of cayenne pepper**
  For the coleslaw:
- **2 carrots, peeled into ribbons**
- **Half a small red cabbage, shredded**
- **4tbsp crème fraîche**
- **Juice of 1 lime**
- **3 spring onions, chopped**
- **1tsp black sesame seeds**

1 Heat the air fryer to 190°C/375°F. Wrap 3 slices of pancetta around each chicken breast, spray with oil and air fry for 10 minutes, turning half way through.

2 For the coleslaw, mix the carrot and red cabbage with the crème fraîche and lime juice, put into a serving bowl and top with the spring onions and sesame seeds

3 For the barbecue sauce, combine all the ingredients in a small pan and mix together. Bring to the boil then simmer for a few minutes. Put the chicken into a serving dish, pour over the hot sauce and sprinkle over the cheese to melt. Serve with coleslaw.

"Hot sauce, melted cheese and chicken – heaven!"

Spiced lamb flatbreads with a herby yoghurt

Baharat is a Middle Eastern spice blend, and it's a fantastic way of adding an instant Lebanese taste to a dish.

Serves 4 • Ready in 20 minutes

- 400g (14oz) lamb loin fillet
- 1tbsp baharat spice mix
- 2tbsp olive oil
- 2 small red onions, peeled and cut into 8 chunks
- 1 aubergine, cut into bite-sized pieces
- 4 flatbreads or pitta breads
- 1 pomegranate, seeds scooped out
- Pickled gherkins, to serve
- 1 lemon, cut into wedges
  For the yoghurt topping:
- 2tbsp tahini
- 8tbsp natural yoghurt
- 2tsp sumac
- 15g (½oz) dill, finely chopped, plus extra to garnish
- Zest of 1 lemon
- 5g (¼oz) mint, leaves chopped
  You will need:
- 6 metal skewers

1 Mix the ingredients for the yoghurt topping together.
2 Slice the lamb into thickish pieces, around 1cm (½in). Heat the air fryer to 180°C/350°F. Mix the baharat spice mix and the olive oil in a large bowl, then toss through the lamb, onions and aubergine and thread onto skewers. Air fry the skewers for 3-5 mins, depending how pink you like your lamb. Remove to a plate; heat the flatbreads in the switched off air fryer for a couple of minutes.
3 Pull the lamb and vegetables off the skewers and pile onto the flatbreads. Spoon over the yoghurt and top with the pomegranate seeds, pickles and extra dill. Serve with lemon wedges.

"This tender lamb dish makes for a healthy, satisfying lunch"

Cheat's steak Béarnaise with rosemary fries

This bistro classic comes together in a flash, thanks to some basic cupboard staples.

Serves 2 • Ready in 15 minutes

- 2 thin-cut sirloin or minute steaks – each about 150g (5oz)
- 1tbsp olive oil
- 250g (9oz) French fry (skinny) oven chips
- 2tsp finely chopped rosemary
- Zest of ½ lemon
- 1tsp flaked sea salt
- Watercress or rocket, to serve
  For the Béarnaise sauce:
- 4tbsp mayonnaise
- 2tbsp full-fat crème fraîche
- 2tsp wholegrain mustard
- ½tsp white wine vinegar
- Squeeze of lemon juice
- 1-2tbsp roughly chopped fresh tarragon leaves

1 Mix all the Béarnaise sauce ingredients together in a bowl and season with a pinch of salt and black pepper.
2 Heat the air fryer to 180°C/350°F. Rub the steaks with oil, air fry for 2 minutes a side. Set aside to rest.
3 Turn up the air fryer to 200°C/400°F and air fry the oven chips for 8 minutes, or until well browned, shaking the basket a few times.
4 Rub the rosemary and lemon zest into the flaky salt, then toss with the steak.
5 Serve the steaks with a big dollop of the Béarnaise sauce, fries and watercress on the side.

> "A juicy steak with fries is a winner every time"

Korean barbecue chicken & waffles

Chicken and waffles is a classic American soul-food pairing, but we've given it a Korean spin. Do buy the waffles if you don't have a waffle maker or want to save time.

Serves 6-8 • Ready in 45 minutes plus marinating

- 8 x skin-on boneless chicken thighs
  For the marinade:
- 350g (12oz) Korean BBQ sauce
- 2tbsp gochujang
- 4cm (1½in) piece of fresh ginger, peeled and grated
- 1 garlic clove, minced
  For the waffles:
- 250g (9oz) plain flour
- 2tbsp caster sugar
- 2tsp baking powder
- 1tsp bicarbonate of soda
- 1tsp salt
- 425g (15oz) buttermilk
- 2 eggs
- 100g (3½oz) unsalted butter, melted
  For the pickled cucumber:
- 1tbsp soy sauce
- 2tbsp mirin or rice vinegar
- 1tbsp sugar
- 1tsp gochugaru (or any chilli flakes), plus extra to garnish
- 2 spring onions, chopped
- 4 small pickling cucumbers, thinly sliced
- 1tsp sesame seeds
- Sriracha mayo, to serve

1 Mix all the marinade ingredients in a large bowl and add in the chicken. Leave the mixture in the fridge overnight.
2 For the waffles, sieve the dry ingredients together. Whisk together the buttermilk and eggs, and stir into the dry ingredients, followed by the melted butter.
3 Heat a waffle maker. Ladle the batter in the centre, close the lid and cook for 5 mins, or until golden. Keep warm in the oven.
4 For the pickled cucumber, mix the soy sauce, mirin, sugar and chilli flakes together, then add in the spring onions – reserving a few for garnish – and cucumber, and sprinkle over half the sesame seeds.
5 Heat the air fryer to 200°C/400°F. Take the chicken out of the marinade and leave at air temperature while the air fryer is heating up. Put the chicken on to a silicone or parchment liner. Air fry for 7 minutes, then turn over and cook for a further 7 minutes. Check it's cooked through by inserting a skewer into the thickest part, or it's at 75°C/167°F with a meat thermometer.
6 To serve, layer the waffles with sriracha mayo and place the cucumbers on top. Add the chicken and a scattering of spring onions and remaining sesame seeds.

Cantonese-style crispy pork with noodles

The air fryer makes easy work of pork belly with a perfect result every time.

Serves 4 • Ready in 1 hour plus overnight chilling

- 2tbsp rice wine vinegar, plus extra for brushing
- 1tsp Chinese five-spice powder
- 1tbsp brown sugar
- ½tsp smoked sea salt
- 1 garlic clove, grated
- 1kg (2¼lb) piece pork belly
- Oil spray
  For the spicy noodles:
- 600g 1¼lb) fresh egg noodles
- 2tsp crispy chilli oil
- 1tbsp sesame seed oil
- Juice of 1 lime
- Small handful coriander, roughly chopped
- Roasted peanuts and sliced red chilli, to garnish (optional)

1 The night before, mix together the rice wine vinegar, five spice, sugar, smoked sea salt and garlic. Rub over the pork meat but do not put any on the pork skin. Transfer to a dish or container. Pat the skin dry and use a sharp knife to pierce all over. The more little holes the better. Be careful not to cut too deep, as you don't want to reach the layer of fat below the skin. Brush with a little rice wine vinegar. Leave in the fridge uncovered overnight.
2 Heat the air fryer to 200°C/400°F. Spray the skin of the pork with oil, and grind over some sea salt. Air fry for 25 minutes, reduce the temperature to 160°C/300°F and cook for a further 30 minutes. Leave on a board to rest.
3 Meanwhile, cook the noodles according to the pack instructions then toss together with the oils, lime juice and coriander. Transfer to a serving bowl and garnish with peanuts and red chilli, if using. Slice the pork and serve with the noodles.

Lamb cutlets with pea & mint purée

Lamb cutlets, cut from the rack, are small and quite thin, so they cook very quickly.

Serves 4 • Ready in 30 minutes

- 2 garlic cloves, crushed
- Juice of 1 lemon
- 2tbsp olive oil
- 8 lamb cutlets
- 2 baby globe artichokes
- 250g (9oz) frozen peas
- ½ small pack fresh mint, the leaves picked
- 5tbsp crème fraîche
- ½ pack of chives
- Juice of ½ lemon

1 In a non-metallic bowl, mix the garlic, lemon juice and half the oil, add the lamb cutlets and set aside to marinate. Heat the air fryer to 200°C/400°F.

2 Bring a pan of salted water to the boil and cook the artichokes for 10-15 mins until tender and a knife can be placed through them. Cut them into quarters, drizzle over the remaining oil. Air fry 3 minutes until crisp and tender.

3 In a heatproof bowl, cover the peas with just-boiled water and leave to stand for 2 mins. Drain, then add to a food processor with the mint, crème fraîche, chives, lemon juice and seasoning. Whizz until smooth and adjust the seasoning.

4 Air fry the cutlets for 4-6 minutes, depending how you like your lamb, turning once. Warm the purée through and serve with the lamb and artichokes.

"Save time and buy a jar of small, cooked artichokes in oil"

Steak with courgette tzatziki

Leaving steaks to rest once cooked ensures the juices stay put, for a perfectly tender steak.

Serves 4 • Ready in 20 minutes

- **2 large courgettes**
- **4 x 225g (8oz) sirloin steaks**
- **Oil spray**
  For the tzatziki:
- **1 bunch mint, finely chopped**
- **1 bunch basil, finely chopped**
- **1 bunch dill, finely chopped**
- **4tsp strong horseradish sauce**
- **2tbsp Dijon mustard**
- **200g (7oz) mixture half yoghurt, half crème fraîche**
  To serve:
- **Watercress or rocket leaves**
- **Fried potato slices or wedges**

1 Prick the courgettes and place them under a very hot grill until just charred. Remove from the heat, then when cool, finely chop them.
2 Heat the air fryer to 180°C/350°F. Spray the steaks with oil and season. Air fry for 8 minutes, turning half way through, for medium rare. Leave to rest.
3 Mix together all the ingredients for the tzatziki, season well and stir in the chopped courgettes.
4 Serve the steaks with the tzatziki and potato slices.

Cook's Tip
Make the potatoes in the air fryer, too, by tossing slices in oil and salt, then air fry at 200°C/400°F for 10 minutes, shaking halfway.

Warm chicken & grain salad with green harissa

Pouches of healthy pre-cooked grains work so well in salads. Simply choose your favourite for this punchy recipe.

Serves 2-3 • Ready in 15 minutes

- 6 chicken mini fillets
- 2tbsp olive oil
- 3tbsp za'atar
- 1 courgette, thinly sliced into coins
- 3 spring onions, finely sliced
- 250g (9oz) pouch pre-cooked mixed grains
- 30g (1oz) flaked almonds, toasted
- Small bunch mint or coriander, roughly chopped
- Finely grated zest and juice of 1 lemon

For the green harissa:
- 1 garlic clove
- 2 spring onions, roughly chopped
- Large handful mixed soft herbs, leaves picked (we used a mix of parsley, coriander, mint and basil)
- 2 green chillies, seeds scraped
- Juice of ½ lemon
- 1tsp ground cumin
- 1tsp ground coriander
- 60ml (4tbsp) olive oil

1 Heat the air fryer to 190°C/375°F. Toss the chicken with 1tbsp oil, 2tbsp za'atar and some salt. Air fry for 4-5 minutes, turning once, until browned and cooked through. Set aside.
2 For the green harissa, blitz all the ingredients in a food processor until finely chopped. Season with salt and more lemon juice if needed. Set aside.
3 Meanwhile, heat the remaining oil in a pan over a high heat. Add the courgette and cook for 2 mins until beginning to colour. Add the spring onion, grains and almonds, then cook for 1-2 mins more until warmed through. Stir through the herbs, lemon and the remaining za'atar. Season and add more oil and lemon to your taste.
4 Pile the chicken and grain salad onto a serving platter. Sprinkle over the remaining almonds and drizzle with 3tbsp harissa. Serve with lemon wedges.

Pork schnitzel with winter slaw

Air fryer schnitzels are the best! Crunchy, crisp and tender, with no oil at all.

Serves 4 • Ready in 20 minutes

- **4 pork loin steaks**
- **60g (2oz) plain flour, seasoned**
- **2 eggs, beaten**
- **90g (3oz) breadcrumbs**
- **½ lemon, cut into wedges, to serve**
  For the winter slaw:
- **¼ red cabbage, sliced**
- **½ bulb fennel, sliced**
- **2tbsp crème fraîche**
- **1tsp Dijon mustard**
- **Juice ½ lemon**

1 To make the winter slaw, mix the veg with the crème fraîche, mustard and lemon juice. Season and set aside.

2 Place the pork steaks one by one between two sheets of clingfilm. Use a rolling pin to thin them evenly out to just under 5mm (¼in).

3 Tip the flour, egg and breadcrumbs onto three separate plates. Coat the meat in the flour, then the egg and, finally, the breadcrumbs.

4 Heat the air fryer to 180°C/350°F. Air fry the schnitzels for 10 minutes – you may need to do this in two batches. Serve with the winter slaw.

"Crisp, tender pork schnitzels are perfect cooked in the air fryer"

Cook's Tip
Remember if you need to air fry in batches, you can always pop the first ones back into the air fryer for a minute or two to reheat fully.

Sticky chicken drumsticks

For an alternative roast we love chicken drumsticks served with a side of fresh coleslaw. Bonus points for serving with homemade fries!

Serves 4 • Ready in 20 minutes

- **4tbsp honey**
- **4tbsp soy sauce**
- **4tbsp tomato ketchup**
- **8 chicken drumsticks**
  For the slaw:
- **2tsp black sesame seeds**
- **2tbsp rice wine vinegar**
- **3tbsp soy sauce**
- **2tsp sesame oil**
- **1tsp sugar**
- **4 carrots, thinly sliced**
- **2 cucumbers, thinly sliced**
- **6 spring onions, thinly sliced**
- **1 chilli, thinly sliced**

1 Heat the air fryer to 200°C/400°F. Combine the honey, soy sauce and tomato ketchup in a large mixing bowl.
2 Slash the skins of the drumsticks and add to the bowl, tossing to coat in the sauce. Air fry on a silicon liner for 12 minutes, turning once.
3 Combine the sesame seeds, vinegar, soy, sesame oil, sugar in a mixing bowl, then add the remaining ingredients, tossing well.
Serve the chicken with the slaw.

Cook's Tip
For extra flavour leave the chicken to marinate overnight.

Cook's Tip
Take the chicken out of the fridge 30 mins before cooking to allow it to reach room temperature; this will allow it to cook more evenly.

Roast chicken Caesar salad

As a general rule, a whole chicken under 1.5kg (3½lb) will fit into the basket of most air fryers. The result, in less time, gives a succulent bird with crisp skin.

Serves 4 • Ready in 1 hour

- 6 anchovies, mashed to a paste
- 1 whole garlic bulb, plus 2 extra cloves, finely grated
- 5tbsp mayonnaise
- 2tbsp Dijon mustard, plus more for serving
- 2tbsp olive oil
- 1.5kg (3½lb) whole chicken
- 2 lemons, zest and juice 1
- 200g (7oz) bread, torn into bite-size chunks
- 6 rashers cooked crisp streaky bacon
- 2tbsp Parmesan, finely grated, plus extra shaved to serve
- 2 romaine hearts, leaves separated, torn

1 Heat the air fryer to 180°C/350°F. Mix together the anchovies, grated garlic, 3tbsp mayonnaise, 1tbsp mustard, 1tbsp oil, and plenty of ground black pepper until smooth.
2 Season the chicken all over, inside and out. Halve one lemon and stuff in the cavity. Set aside 1tbsp of the anchovy mayo, then rub the rest over the chicken.
3 Wrap the whole garlic bulb in foil. Put the chicken in the air fryer and tuck in the garlic. Add a small cup of water. Air fry for 40 minutes, then remove and leave the chicken to rest. Check it's cooked through by piercing the thickest part of the thigh – the juices should run clear.
4 Pour any juices from the air fryer into a small ovenproof dish which fits the air fryer. Squeeze out the garlic and add half to the dish, with the bread. Air fry for 3-5 minutes or until crisp.
5 Meanwhile, mix the remaining roasted garlic, mayo, mustard, oil, lemon zest and juice, reserved anchovy mixture and Parmesan in a large bowl. Season to taste, then toss in the romaine. Break up the bacon and add to the salad bowl, along with the crispy croutons, then transfer to a serving platter. Carve the chicken and add to the serving platter. Shave over some extra Parmesan to serve.

Crumbed pork chop, Thai-style

A simple pork chop is transformed with a nutty, spicy and sweet topping.

Serves 2 • Ready in 30 minutes

- 2 pork chops
- Oil spray
  For the crispy topping:
- 4tbsp breadcrumbs
- 1tbsp dried sage
- Knob of melted butter
  For the salad:
- ½ cucumber, de-seeded and sliced into half moons
- 1 red onion thinly sliced
- ¼ white cabbage, thinly sliced
- 30g (1oz) pomegranate seeds
- 50g (1½oz) peanuts
  For the dressing:
- 2tbsp soy
- 2tbsp fish sauce
- 2tbsp honey
- 2tbsp sesame seed oil
- 2tbsp chilli sauce
- 2tbsp water
- Juice 1 lime
- 2tbsp crispy onions, to serve (optional)
- Black sesame seeds, to serve (optional)

1 Heat the air fryer to 180°C/350°F. Combine all of the salad ingredients in a big bowl. Mix together the dressing ingredients in a separate bowl, toss together and set aside.
2 Combine the breadcrumbs and dried sage with a ½ knob of melted butter and seasoning. Spray the chops with oil, then air fry for 5 minutes. Turn, then press on the breadcrumb mixture, spreading it evenly, and air fry for a further 5 minutes until cooked through and the crumbs are crisp.
3 Toss the salad ingredients with the dressing and serve with the pork chops.

Spanish chicken skewers with patatas bravas

These simple and delicious skewers are ideal for sharing with friends.

Serves 8 • Ready in 1 hr 10 mins, plus marinating

For the chicken:
- 8 skinless, boneless chicken thighs, cut into 3cm (1.2in) pieces
- 2tbsp olive oil
- 4 garlic cloves, crushed
- 100ml (3½fl oz) dry sherry
- 2tbsp honey

For the patatas bravas:
- 5tbsp olive oil
- 1kg (2¼lb) waxy potatoes, peeled and cut into 2cm (¾in) pieces
- 2 garlic cloves, crushed
- ½ red chilli, finely chopped
- 250g (9oz) passata
- ½tbsp tomato purée
- 1tbsp sherry vinegar
- 1tsp paprika (smoked or sweet)
- ½tsp caster sugar
- Mayonnaise, to serve

You will need:
- 8 metal skewers

1 Toss the chicken pieces with the oil, garlic, sherry and honey. Marinate for 30 mins or overnight in the fridge. Thread the chicken onto the skewers.

2 Heat the air fryer to 190°C/375°F. Spray the basket with oil. Toss the potatoes and garlic in 1tbsp olive oil, then air fry for 10 minutes. Shake well, increase the temperature to 200°C/400°F, then air fry for a further 5 minutes.

3 Meanwhile, heat the remaining oil in a pan and cook the garlic and chilli for 2 mins. Add the passata, tomato purée, vinegar, paprika and sugar with plenty of seasoning and cook for 10 mins.

4 Set the potatoes to one side – you can quickly reheat them in the air fryer for a minute or two to serve. Air fry the skewers for 10 minutes.

5 To serve, spread the sauce over the base of a serving platter or plates, spread over the potatoes, drizzle with mayonnaise and top with the chicken.

Greek roast chicken gyros

A healthy roast with a difference, herby chicken served with toasted pittas and plenty of salad. Our top tip? Make a little "dish" with foil to put under the chicken in the base of the air fryer to catch all the juices.

Serves 4 • Ready in 1 hour plus marinating

- 6 garlic cloves, peeled and crushed
- 2tbsp dried oregano
- 100ml (3½ fl oz) olive oil
- Juice and rind of 1 lemon
- 2tsp cumin seeds
- 1.5kg (3lb) whole, free-range chicken
- Tzatziki, pitta breads and Greek salad to serve
- A few dill sprigs, to serve

1 Whisk together the garlic, oregano, olive oil, lemon juice and rind and cumin seeds. Rub all over the chicken and leave to marinate in a large roasting tin for at least 15 mins or overnight.

2 Heat the air fryer to 180°C/350°F. Air fry the chicken breast-side up for 30 minutes, then turn over and air fry for a further 15 minutes. Check that the juices run clear when thickest part of the thigh is pierced with a skewer.

3 To serve, pull the meat off the carcass and add any of the roasting juices from the pan of the air fryer. Let everyone make up their own pitta pockets with tzatziki and salad.

Salmon with parmesan and fennel crust

With a few ingredients, this air-fried salmon dish will give a flavoursome, juicy meal in no time at all.

Serves 6 • Ready in 15 minutes

- 1 bulb fennel, finely sliced
- 1tbsp extra virgin olive oil
- 75g (3oz) breadcrumbs
- 100g (4oz) Parmesan, finely grated
- 6 salmon fillets
- Olive oil spray

1 Heat the air fryer to 180°C/350°F. Bring a small pan of salted water to the boil, add the fennel slices and cook for 1 or 2 minutes. Rinse in cold water, drain and set aside to dry on kitchen towel.

2 Mix the fennel, olive oil, breadcrumbs and half the Parmesan with some seasoning, use to coat the salmon fillets and top with the remaining Parmesan. Spray lightly with oil, then press the Parmesan down with a fish slice – this keeps it "glued" down or it may be dislodged with the power of the fan. Put the fish on to a silicone mat or parchment lining to prevent sticking. Air fry for 10 minutes. Depending on the size of the salmon fillets, this may need to be done in two batches. Serve with new potatoes and green beans.

Cook's Tip
This recipe would work equally well with any white, meaty fish, such as hake or cod.

Gourmet fish finger & tartare sarnie

Once you've made an air-fried homemade fish finger, you'll never look back! So light and crisp, without a hint of oil required.

Serves 2 • Ready in 20 minutes

- 200g (7oz) skinless, boneless cod fillets, cut into thick strips
- 2tbsp plain four, seasoned
- 75g (2½oz) breadcrumbs
- Zest of 2 lemons
- 1 egg, beaten
- 1 mini ciabatta or bread roll, halved
- Rocket leaves
  For the tartare sauce:
- 2tbsp mayonnaise
- 3 gherkins, chopped
- 1tbsp parsley, roughly chopped
- 1tsp lemon juice

1 Mix together all the ingredients for the tartare sauce and set aside.
2 Heat the air fryer to 180°C/350°F. Put the fish pieces into a large bowl and add the four. Toss together until the fish pieces are well coated. In a separate bowl, mix together the breadcrumbs and lemon zest.
3 Dip each piece in the beaten egg, then in the breadcrumbs to coat. Air fry, spacing them a little apart, for 7 minutes.
4 Slice and toast the ciabatta, spread over the mayonnaise, sprinkle with rocket and top with fish fingers to serve.

Salmon in a parcel

Traditionally, this healthy method of baking fish sees it wrapped in parchment paper, but foil works better in an air fryer because of the weight, which stops it flapping around in the powerful fan.

Serves 4 • Ready in 30 minutes

- 4 medium purple or white potatoes
- 1 large bulb fennel, thinly sliced
- 4 salmon fillets, skin on
- 1tsp sea salt flakes
- 1tsp coarse black pepper
- 1tbsp olive oil, plus extra for brushing
- 1 large red onion, chopped
- 20g (¾oz) unsalted butter
- 4 garlic cloves, roughly crushed
- 200ml (7fl oz) dark rum or white wine
- 1 lemon, quartered, to serve

1 Boil the potatoes for 15mins, drain and, when cool, slice into rounds 2cm (0.8in) thick.

3 Score the skin of each fish and pack the holes/cuts with salt and pepper. Brush the skin with the oil and flash-fry (less than 1min) skin-side down in a dry, super-hot pan just to crisp the skin. Heat the air fryer to 180°C/350°F.

4 Take four pieces of foil, and brush lightly with oil. Make a small pile of potatoes, fennel, onion, butter, fennel fronds and garlic, all divided up evenly, in the centre of each piece of foil. Pour equal parts of rum or white wine on to each pile and place the salmon on top. Scrunch up the centre of foil to seal, leaving a bit of space below, but not too high that it will reach the heating element of the air fryer.

5 Air fry for 10 minutes – you may need to do this in two batches, depending on the size of the salmon. Put the parcels onto serving plates and allow everyone to open their own.

Soy-marinated cod skewers with baby pak choi

It's worth investing in the perfect-sized metal skewers for your air fryer, as anything on a stick, whether meat, fish or poultry, cooks so quickly. Perfect for when the barbecue isn't an option.

Serves 6 • Ready in 45 mins

- **600g (1 ¼lb) thick cod loin**
  For the marinade:
- **3tbsp sesame seed oil**
- **3tbsp dark soy**
- **1tbsp lime juice**
- **1tbsp honey**
- **1tsp dried chilli flakes**
  For the skewers:
- **6 baby pak choi**
- **6 spring onions**
  To serve:
- **1 fresh red chilli, sliced (optional)**
- **Fresh lime wedges**
  You will need:
- **6 metal skewers**
- **Oil spray**

1 Cut the cod into 24 chunks. In a bowl mix the marinade ingredients, stir in the cod and leave for 30 mins.
2 Cut the pak choi in half lengthways and slice the spring onions into thirds. Finely chop the leafy green part and reserve for garnish. Slice the remaining spring onion in half lengthways. Heat the air fryer to 180°C/350°F.
3 On a skewer, thread four chunks of cod and either four halves of pak choi or four pieces of spring onion. Brush a little marinade on the veg.
4 Spritz the skewers with oil, then air fry for 5 minutes, turning once. Serve with the spring onion, chilli and extra soy.

97

Pilchard fish cakes

A simple, budget-friendly and healthy fish cake with a crisp crumb.

Serves 4 · Ready in 30 minutes

- **450g (1lb) potatoes, peeled and cut into chunks**
- **400g (14oz) tin pilchards in tomato sauce (reserve sauce for the dip)**
- **Zest and juice of one lemon, plus lemon wedges to serve**
- **½ bunch parsley, chopped**
- **1 bunch chives, finely chopped**
- **1 small onion, finely chopped**
- **1 egg, beaten**
- **4tbsp breadcrumbs**
- **Oil spray**
  For the dipping sauce:
- **3tbsp crème fraiche or soured cream**
- **3tbsp mayonnaise**

1 Steam the potatoes for 15 mins or until cooked through. In a large bowl, roughly mash with a fork. Heat the air fryer to 200°C/400°F.
2 Drain the pilchards, reserving 3tbsp of the tomato sauce for the dipping sauce, then mix the fish into the mashed potato with lemon zest and juice, herbs and onion, and stir until well combined. Form mixture into 4 fishcakes. Dip in beaten egg, then in breadcrumbs, to coat. Spray with oil.
3 Air fry the fishcakes for 10 minutes, until crisp and browned. To make the sauce, mix together the cream and mayo with the reserved tomato sauce. Serve with the hot fish cakes and the lemon wedges.

Roasted new potato and salmon salad

Roasting baby new potatoes in an air fryer means less time, with a crisp, tender potato in just 20 minutes.

Serves 4 • Ready in 45 minutes

- **450g (1lb)) baby new potatoes, halved**
- **1 garlic clove, crushed**
- **2tbsp olive oil**
- **100g (3½oz) pistachio nuts**
- **¼tsp sea salt**
- **200g (7oz) green beans, trimmed**
- **125g (4oz) watercress, rocket and spinach**
- **200g (7oz) hot smoked salmon, flaked**
- **200g (7oz) radishes, trimmed and sliced**

For the dressing:
- **2tbsp extra virgin olive oil**
- **1tbsp white wine vinegar**
- **1tbsp maple syrup**
- **1tsp Dijon mustard**

1 Heat the air fryer to 200°C/400°F. Toss the potatoes in the garlic and oil, air fry for 20 minutes.

2 Add the pistachios to the potatoes for the last 2 minutes of cooking.

3 Blanch the green beans in salted water; drain.

4 Arrange the watercress, rocket and spinach on a platter. Top with the potatoes, pistachios, beans, flaked salmon and radishes. Put the dressing ingredients in a jar with 2tbsp water and season. Seal and shake to mix. Serve with the salad.

Tikka salmon kebabs with minty yoghurt

A speedy lunch for one – it's worth allowing a little time for the salmon to marinate for maximum flavour. These are best air-fried on a silicone mat.

Serves 1 · Ready in 10 minutes plus marinating

- **1 salmon fillet, cut into 2cm (¾in) cubes**
- **1 red onion, cut into wedges**
- **2tbsp tikka curry paste**
- **3tbsp natural yoghurt**
- **½ lemon**
- **¼ cucumber, diced**
- **Few mint leaves, roughly chopped**
- **Oil spray**
- **Naan bread, to serve**

1 Thread your salmon onto two metal skewers, alternating with the onion wedges. Mix the tikka paste with 1tbsp of the yoghurt and a good squeeze of lemon juice, and spread onto your kebabs. Leave to marinate for 15 mins. Heat the air fryer to 180°C/350°F.

2 To make the minty yoghurt, mix together the remaining yoghurt with the cucumber and mint leaves. Season to taste.

3 Spray the skewers with a little oil, then air fry for 7 minutes, turning once. Serve with the minty yoghurt and naan bread, or other flat bread of your choice.

Cook's Tip
The salmon is perfect served with some buttery new potatoes on the side.

Salmon parcels with fennel and citrus

Pernod, an aniseed spirit, works well with the fennel, but you can use white wine or vermouth instead.

Serves 4 · Ready in 40 minutes

- 2 bulbs of fennel (core removed), sliced (save the fronds for garnish)
- 3 shallots, peeled and sliced
- Oil spray
- 40g (1 ½oz) butter, diced
- 3tbsp Pernod
- 1tbsp white wine
- Handful fresh parsley, chopped
- 350g (12oz) piece salmon fillet
- 1 red grapefruit, cut into segments

1 Blanch the fennel in a pan of salted water. Drain and plunge into iced water. Heat the air fryer to 200°C/400°F.

2 Take a piece of foil, large enough to wrap the salmon in, and spray with oil. Put the fennel and shallots in the centre. Pull up the edges so the liquid doesn't pour out. Dot cubes of butter over the vegetables, pour over the Pernod and wine and scatter with half the parsley. Place the salmon on top. Season.

3 Scrunch up the sides and seal the top, leaving a gap for air to circulate but not so high as the foil touches the element. Air fry for 30 minutes, checking the thickest part of the salmon is cooked as you like it.

4 Transfer to a large plate or board, rip open the paper and scatter over the grapefruit, along with the remaining parsley. Garnish with fennel fronds.

Filo fish pies

The filling for these individual pies needs to be hot before going into the air fryer, or the filo may over-brown.

Serves 6 • Ready in 35 minutes

For the filling:
- **300ml (10fl oz) semi-skimmed milk**
- **2 bay leaves**
- **200g (7oz) hake, cut into chunks**
- **200g (7oz) smoked haddock, cut into chunks**
- **200g (7oz) salmon, cut into chunks**
- **1 onion, finely chopped**
- **2tbsp butter**
- **2tbsp flour**
- **1tsp English mustard**
- **125g (4½oz) peas**
- **1 bunch of dill, roughly chopped**
- **4 cooked beetroot, cut into wedges**

For the topping:
- **6 sheets of filo pastry**
- **25g (1oz) butter, melted**
- **Green salad and lemon wedges, to serve**

You will need:
- **6 ramekins**

1 For the filling, heat the milk and bay leaves. Poach all the fish for 3-4mins in the liquid, then remove. Drain off the milk, reserving it for the sauce. Rinse out the pan. Heat the air fryer to 180°C/350°F.

2 Fry the onion in the butter, then add the flour and the milk, whisking until the mixture has thickened. Stir in the mustard, fish, peas, dill and beetroot and heat through gently.

3 Divide between the ramekins. You may need to cook these in two batches, depending on the size of your air fryer. Brush the filo with melted butter and top each ramekin with a sheet of crumpled filo. Air fry for 10 minutes, until the filo is golden brown. Serve with salad and lemon wedges.

Sweet potato & courgette fish cakes

These make a delicious lunch or light dinner but you could make mini versions for parties or to serve as a starter.

Serves 4 • Ready in 35 minutes

- **1 sweet potato, approx 250g (9oz) , pricked with a fork**
- **2 baking potatoes, approx, 450g (1lb), pricked with a fork**
- **1 small courgette, approx 200g (7oz) , grated**
- **225g (8oz) skinless, boneless white fish, cut into 4cm (1½in) pieces (eg cod or hake)**
- **1 lime, zest and half the juice**
- **3tbsp breadcrumbs, plus 3tbsp for coating**
- **2 eggs, beaten**
- **1tsp dried chilli flakes**
- **Oil spray**
- **Tenderstem broccoli to serve (optional)**
- **Spicy mayonnaise or hot sauce to serve (optional)**

1 Prick the sweet potato and potatoes a few times with a fork. Cook in the microwave, on high, for 10–15 mins until soft.
2 Meanwhile, put the courgette in a sieve and squeeze firmly to remove the excess moisture, then put in a bowl and mix with the cod, lime zest and juice, 50g (2oz) breadcrumbs, eggs and chilli until combined.
3 Once cool enough to handle, peel the cooked potatoes and add the flesh to the cod mixture. Season and mix well to mash up the potato. Heat the air fryer to 180°C/350°F.
4 Put the remaining breadcrumbs on a plate. Divide the fish cake mix into 8 equal portions. Squeeze into a ball in your hands then coat in the breadcrumbs. Flatten to make 7-8cm (2.7-3in) patties.
5 Spray the air fryer basket with oil, then air fry the fishcakes for 15 minutes, flipping half way through and spraying again with oil. Serve with a squeeze of lime, broccoli, and spicy mayo, if you like.

Jerk salmon with mango yoghurt

Salmon is a rich, oily fish which absorbs spicy flavours so well. If you don't have a spiraliser, simply buy spiralled vegetables instead.

Serves 4 • Ready in 30 minutes, plus marinating

- **1tbsp jerk seasoning**
- **7tbsp thick yoghurt (0% fat is fine)**
- **4 skinned salmon fillets**
- **450g (1lb) sweet potato, peeled**
- **400g (14oz) courgette, trimmed**
- **1 mango, diced**
- **Juice of 1 lime**
- **1tbsp fresh mint**
- **Oil spray**

1 Mix the jerk seasoning with 2tbsp of yoghurt. Put the salmon in a shallow dish and coat with the yoghurt mix. Cover and chill in the fridge. You can leave it overnight if you have time, but it's still delicious if left for just half an hour.
2 Spiralise the vegetables. Put the sweet potato into a microwavable dish with a splash of water. Mix the mango, lime juice, mint and remaining yoghurt with plenty of seasoning. Heat the air fryer to 180°C/350°F. Add a silicone mat and spray with oil. Put the salmon into the air fryer, spray and air fry for 10 minutes.

3 Meanwhile, microwave the sweet potatoes on high for 3 mins, remove and stir in the courgettes. Add a drizzle of olive oil and seasoning. Serve the salmon on the veg with the remaining yoghurt on top.

"Salmon pairs so well with spicy, punchy flavours"

Miso spiced fish skewers

A miso glaze turns an ordinary fish skewer into something a bit more punchy. Togarashi powder (7 Spice Seasoning) is found in most supermarkets, and adds a chilli buzz.

Serves 2 • Ready in 10 minutes, plus marinating

For the marinade:
- 2tbsp miso paste
- 1tbsp mirin
- Pinch chilli powder
- Half a lemon
- 2 x 150g (5oz) firm white fish fillets, each thickly sliced into 3
- Oil spray

For the dressing:
- 3tbsp crème fraîche
- ½tsp togarashi powder

To serve:
- Wedge of red cabbage, sliced
- 1 head red chicory, leaves removed
- Lemon wedges
- Thai basil, optional, to serve

1 To make the marinade, mix together the miso, mirin, chilli powder and a squeeze of lemon juice. Rub over the fish, and thread each piece on to a metal skewer. Leave to marinate for 10-20 mins. Heat the air fryer to 180°C/350°F.

2 For the dressing, combine the crème fraîche, a squeeze of lemon juice and the togarashi powder.

3 Spray the skewers with oil. Air fry on a silicone liner for 4-5 minutes, turning halfway through. Divide the cabbage and chicory leaves between two plate, drizzle with the dressing, add the fish skewers and serve with lemon wedges and Thai basil.

Crab & sweetcorn cakes

Makes 4 • Ready in 25 minutes, plus chilling

- 300g (11oz) crabmeat: ½ brown, ½ white
- 150g (5oz) sweetcorn kernels
- 4tbsp fresh breadcrumbs, plus extra to coat
- 2tbsp mayonnaise
- 1 chilli, finely chopped
- 1tbsp Thai fish sauce
- Zest and juice of 2 limes
- 3 spring onions, finely sliced
- 1 bunch coriander, finely chopped
- Oil spray
- Chilli dipping sauce and lime wedges, to serve

1 Mix together the crabmeat, sweetcorn, breadcrumbs, mayonnaise, chilli, fish sauce, lime zest and juice, spring onions and coriander. Shape into four crab cakes, then carefully dip them into the breadcrumbs. Put them in the fridge for 20-30 mins to firm up.

2 Heat the air fryer to 190°C/375°F. Spray the basket with oil. When it's at temperature, put the crab cakes in the basket and spray. Air fry for 15-17 minutes, flipping half way through and spray again. They should be golden, crisp and piping hot.

3 Serve with the chilli dipping sauce and lime wedges.

Cook's Tip
Frozen sweetcorn is fine for this recipe – just thaw it before using. Canned sweetcorn can make the crab cakes a little wet.

SIDES

p119
The best
homemade
fries ever!

Jacket potatoes

Though they don't take much less time than in an oven, at least you aren't heating a large oven for just one or two jacket potatoes. Our method will give you a crisp skin and a tantalising fluffy centre.

Serves 2 • Ready in 1 hour

- **2 medium potatoes**
- **Olive oil or spray**
- **Sea salt**

Heat the air fryer to 200°C/400°F. Pierce the potatoes with a carving fork or metal skewer. Rub with oil, then grind over plenty of sea salt. Air fry for 1 hour, turning halfway through.

Try these other tasty fillings:
- **Roasted red peppers with a little feta cheese**
- **Mushrooms sautéed in olive oil with plenty of black pepper**
- **Thick yoghurt with mint, cucumber and coriander**
- **Thick yoghurt mixed with pesto**

Cook's Tip
No need to load with butter! Add some whipped ricotta, then add a little mature Cheddar. Sprinkle over lots of pepper and some chilli flakes.

Roasted sprouts

This method of air-frying sprouts gives a sweet and tender result. Even die-hard sprout-haters will love them!

Serves 4 • Ready in 35 minutes

- **450g (1lb) Brussels sprouts, trimmed**
- **1tbsp olive oil**
- **1tsp sumac or smoked paprika**
- **3tbsp hazelnuts, toasted and chopped**
- **Knob of butter**

Heat the air fryer to 160°C/325°F. Toss the sprouts in the oil, adding plenty of freshly ground black pepper and sea salt. Air fry for 20 minutes. Increase the temperature to 180°C/350°F, and air fry for a further 5-8 minutes, until tender in the centre and browned and crisp on the outside. Stir in the sumac, hazelnuts and butter. Serve immediately.

Roast potatoes

So quick to roast in an air fryer, crisp on the outside and fluffy in the centre.

Serves 4 • Ready in 1 hr 15 minutes

- 750g (1½lb) floury potatoes (eg King Edward, Yukon Gold, russets or Maris Piper)
- 3tbsp olive oil, or melted goose or duck fat

Peel and cut the potatoes into medium chunks. Steam for 5 minutes. Shake them in a colander to rough up the edges. Heat the air fryer to 190°C/375°F. Toss the potatoes thoroughly in the oil, season with sea salt, then air fry for 30 minutes, giving the basket an occasional shake, until golden brown and crisp.

Cook's Tip

As with all ingredients in an air fryer, leave a bit of space in between the fries and don't over-crowd the basket.

French fries

Some models of air fryer have pre-set functions, invariably including one for homemade fries. Otherwise, follow our guidelines.

Serves 4 • Ready in 35 minutes

- 400g (14oz) potatoes
- 1tbsp oil
- Oil spray
- Sea salt

Heat the air fryer to 160°C/325°F. Peel and cut the potatoes into fries. Put into a bowl of iced water for 10 minutes. This helps to release the starch and give a crisper result. Drain, and dry with a tea towel. Toss well in the oil with a good grinding of sea salt . Spray the basket with oil to prevent sticking. Air fry for 15 minutes, shaking a couple of times, then increase the temperature to 200°C/400°F. Air fry for a further 8 minutes, shaking once, and serve.

Salt-baked potatoes with herbs

Salt-baking potatoes causes the moisture to dry out, giving a fluffy, dry potato, which isn't salty at all!

Takes 1 hr 15 mins • Serves 3-4

- **1kg (2¼lb) rock salt**
- **Handful of fresh thyme and rosemary sprigs**
- **Handful of fresh bay leaves**
- **450g (1lb) new potatoes**
- **2tbsp unsalted butter, cubed**

1 Heat the air fryer to 200°C/400°F. Make a foil parcel large enough to hold the potatoes and salt. Spread one-third of the salt in the parcel and scatter over half the herbs. Nestle in the potatoes, top with most of the remaining herbs (reserve a few to garnish) and spread the rest of the salt on top to cover every potato.
2 Air fry about 40 minutes (depending on the size of the potatoes), until a skewer slides into the centre of the largest potato easily.
3 Remove the potatoes from the salt, brushing off as much as possible, then crush them slightly and put in a serving dish. Finish with butter and top with extra herbs.

Yorkshire puddings

The air fryer is perfect for making a small quantity of Yorkshires. You'll need four ramekins or small metal dishes.

Serves 4 • Ready in 30 minutes

- 3tbsp plain flour
- 1 small egg
- 250ml (8fl oz) whole milk
- Oil, for brushing the ramekins

1 Heat the air fryer to 200°C/400°F. Using a whisk or food processor, blend the ingredients together until smooth. Brush the ramekins thoroughly with oil, then heat through in the air fryer for 5 minutes.
2 Divide the batter between the ramekins, and air fry for 20 minutes, until crisp and risen. Serve immediately.

Roasted pumpkin with a walnut, orange & parsley dressing

A sweet, slightly spicy dressing works well with roasted pumpkin or squash.

Serves 4 • Ready in 20 minutes

- 500g (1lb 2oz) pumpkin or butternut squash, cut into 2cm (¾in) slices
- 1tbsp olive oil
  For the dressing:
- 2tbsp walnuts, chopped
- Generous handful flat-leaf parsley, chopped
- 1 garlic clove, finely chopped
- A good pinch of chilli flakes
- 4tbsp olive oil
- Juice and grated zest of 1 small orange

1 Combine all the dressing ingredients and season with salt and pepper to taste. set aside. Heat the air fryer to 180°C/350°F.
2 Toss the pumpkin or squash with the olive oil and seasoning. Air fry for 15 minutes, shaking once during cooking. To serve, arrange the slices on a platter and spoon over some of the dressing. Serve the remaining dressing on the side.

Cook's Tip
Try serving the asparagus with a squeeze of lemon juice, a little butter and some grated Parmesan or crumbled feta cheese.

Roasted asparagus with herb & pickled red onion salad

Such a speedy way to cook asparagus, roasting it in the air fryer adds a little crispness.

Serves 4 • Ready in 10 minutes

- 1 red onion, thinly sliced
- ½tsp salt
- Juice of 1 lemon
- 3tbsp olive oil, plus extra to drizzle
- Handful of parsley leaves
- 1tbsp dill, sprigs only
- 2 bunches asparagus, trimmed

1 Toss the onion with the salt and pour over the lemon juice. Leave to stand for about 15 minutes, until the onions have turned a vivid pink colour, then drain. Stir through 2tbsp olive oil and herbs, then season with salt and black pepper to taste.
2 Heat the air fryer to 190°C/375°F. Toss the asparagus in the 1tbsp oil and season well. Air fry for 7 minutes, depending on the thickness of the stalks, until tender.
3 As soon as they're ready, place them on a serving plate. Scatter over the herbs and pickled red onion and serve.

Polenta chips with almond za'atar salt

Polenta, or cornmeal, is bland on its own, but load it up with seasoning and cheese and air-fried until crisp, it is instantly delicious.

Serves 4 • Ready in 20 minutes plus chilling

For the polenta chips:
- 450ml (15 fl oz) vegetable stock
- 125g (4oz) coarse, quick-cook polenta
- 1tbsp grated Parmesan
- ½tsp salt
- 1tsp freshly ground black pepper
- Olive oil spray

For the almond za'atar salt:
- 50g (3 tbsp) roasted and salted almonds, roughly crushed
- 1tbsp sesame seeds, toasted
- 2tsp dried oregano
- 2tsp ground sumac
- 2tsp cumin seeds, toasted and roughly crushed
- 1tbsp sea salt flakes
- 2tbsp fresh oregano leaves, chopped

1 Line a small baking tin with cling film and set aside. Put the vegetable stock in a medium saucepan and bring up to the boil. Stirring constantly, add the polenta in a steady stream and continue to stir and cook until the mixture thickens. This should take about 2 minutes. Stir in the Parmesan, salt and black pepper. Pour into the lined tin, level the surface and set aside to cool completely for at least 3 hours. This step can be done up to 2 days in advance – keep the polenta covered in the fridge until needed.

2 To make the almond za'atar salt, combine the crushed almonds with the remaining ingredients, except the fresh oregano, and mix well. This mixture can be kept in an airtight container for up to 2 weeks.

3 Heat the air fryer to 200°C/400°F. Cut the polenta into slim 'chips' and spray with oil. Lay them in a single layer in the air fryer (in batches if needed), and air fry for 10 minutes, turning once. Add the oregano to the za'atar and serve with the chips.

123

Cheesy, sage and truffle hasselback potatoes

Well worth the effort for a special meal, these crisp, buttery potatoes will go down a storm.

Serves 6 • Ready in 45 minutes

- **600g (1¼lb) new potatoes**
- **1tbsp olive oil**
- **15g (1tbsp) melted butter, plus extra for frying**
- **10 sage leaves**
- **3tbsp Parmesan, finely grated**
- **1tbsp truffle oil**

1 Heat the air fryer to 180°C/350°F. Slice your potatoes into hasselbacks.
The easiest way to do this is to place the potato between two chopsticks – this way your knife won't go all the way through. Make the slices approximately 3-5mm (0.1-0.2in) apart.
2 Mix the oil and melted butter. Toss the potatoes well in them and season with salt. Air fry, cut side up, for 25 minutes. After 20 minutes,

sprinkle over 1tbsp of cheese.
3 Meanwhile, melt more butter in a frying pan and fry the sage leaves until crisp. Drain on some kitchen towel, until ready to serve.
4 Once the potatoes are cooked, drizzle over the truffle oil and remaining cheese. Spoon into a serving dish and scatter over the crispy sage leaves.

Salad of roast squash with Serrano ham and Manchego

The squash and pumpkin seeds can be roasted a few hours in advance and served at room temperature. The ham and cheese give it a Spanish vibe, but you could use prosciutto and Parmesan instead.

Serves 4 • Ready in 25 minutes

- 600g (1¼lb) butternut or coquina squash, peeled, deseeded and cut into cubes
- 3tbsp olive oil
- 3tbsp squash or pumpkin seeds
- ½ tsp paprika
- 150g (5oz) sliced Serrano ham
- 2 handfuls of watercress (or rocket), thick stems removed
- 45g (1½oz) Manchego cheese, rind removed
  For the dressing:
- 1 garlic clove, peeled and bruised (bashed slightly)
- 2tbsp sherry vinegar
- ½tsp Dijon mustard
- Pinch of caster sugar
- 4tbsp extra virgin olive oil

1 Heat the air fryer to 180°C/350°F. Toss the squash with 2 tablespoons of the olive oil, season generously and air fry for 15 minutes, shaking once during cooking. Set aside to cool to room temperature.

2 Meanwhile, toss the squash or pumpkin seeds with the remaining tablespoon of olive oil, the paprika and a little salt. Spread out on a small baking tin and air fry for about 2 minutes, until lightly toasted.

3 To make the dressing, put the garlic clove, vinegar, mustard, sugar, oil and a little salt and black pepper in a lidded jam jar and shake vigorously. The dressing can be made up to 4 days ahead and kept in the fridge.

4 To serve the salad, gently toss the squash, ham and watercress with the dressing in a large bowl. Shave the cheese over using a vegetable peeler and scatter with the roasted pumpkin seeds to finish.

Roasted parsnips with honey, hazelnuts & truffle oil

Parsnips become sweeter as they roast. These ones, made extra special with the crunch of hazelnuts and luxurious truffle oil, are much quicker to cook in an air fryer rather than a conventional oven.

Serves 4 • Ready in 25 minutes

- 450g (1lb) parsnips, peeled and sliced lengthways into quarters
- Olive oil to drizzle
- 2tbsp runny honey
- ½ bunch of thyme, leaves only
- A handful of hazelnuts, roughly chopped
- A few drops of truffle oil

1 Heat the air fryer to 180°C/350°F. Put the parsnips into a bowl, season with sea salt and pepper, drizzle over some olive oil and 2 tbsp honey. Scatter over the thyme and toss to mix. Air fry for 15 minutes until the parsnips are caramelised. Scatter over the hazelnuts and air fry for a further 2 minutes.

2 Remove and arrange on a serving platter, drizzle over the remaining honey and a few drops of truffle oil. Serve at once.

Hasselback carrots with hazelnut crumble

A fun and elegant way to serve carrots, and the crumble adds great texture.

Serves 6 • Ready in 1 hr

- **500g (1lb 2oz) heritage carrots**
- **1tbsp olive oil**
- **1tbsp maple syrup**
- **1tsp cumin seeds**
  For the crumble:
- **3tbsp whole roasted hazelnuts**
- **2tsp hazelnut oil**
- **1tsp maple syrup**
- **15g(½oz) watercress or rocket**
- **Pinch of salt**

1 Heat the air fryer to 180°C/350°F. Peel the carrots – if any are particularly thick, cut these in half lengthwise. To create the hasselback effect, take a pair of chopsticks and place either side of the carrot. Using a sharp knife, make cuts 3-5mm (0.1-0.2in) apart down the length of the carrot – the chopsticks will prevent you slicing all the way through. Place in a bowl and toss in the oil, maple syrup and cumin seeds. Season. Air fry for 15 mins.
2 Meanwhile, make the crumble by adding all of the ingredients to a food processor and blitz to a crumble. Once the carrots have been removed from the air fryer, sprinkle over the crumble.

Roasted red peppers with goat's cheese

Perfect as a starter, light lunch or supper. Just add a side salad and crusty bread to mop up the juices.

Serves 6 as a side, 3 for a light meal • Ready in 20 minutes

- 3 red peppers, halved, stalks intact
- Olive oil spray
- 3 ripe tomatoes, halved
- 3 garlic cloves, sliced
- 6 anchovies
- Glug of olive oil
- 60g (2oz) goat's cheese, sliced into 3

Heat the air fryer to 180°C/350°F. Spray the peppers with oil. Place half a tomato and a couple of garlic slivers in each. In 3 of the pepper halves, put 2 anchovies. Drizzle with oil, season with black pepper, then air fry for 10 minutes. Switch off the air fryer so there's no fan – this could make the cheese fly away! Add the cheese to the non-anchovy pepper then air fry for 2 more minutes.

Avocado & courgette fries

Crisp fries in a cheesy crumb, minus the deep-frying, work brilliantly in an air fryer.

Serves 4 as a snack • Ready in 15 minutes

- **1 medium egg, beaten**
- **2tbsp plain flour, seasoned**
- **3tbsp panko breadcrumbs, mixed with 3tbsp finely grated Parmesan**
- **1 unripened avocado, sliced lengthways**

1 Heat the air fryer to 190°C/375°F. Put the egg, flour, breadcrumbs and Parmesan mix in three separate bowls.
2 Dip the avocado and courgette slices in flour, shaking off any excess, followed by the egg, then coat in crumbs. Repeat with the rest of the veg. Air fry for 10 minutes, turning once after 6 minutes.
3 Serve alongside some dips.

Swede fries with mustard mayo

Not the most glamorous of vegetables, but swedes do make great low-carb fries.

Serves 4 • Ready in 30 minutes

- **2 swedes (rutabaga), peeled**
- **2tbsp olive oil**
- **½tsp smoked sea salt**
- For the dip:
- **2tbsp low-fat mayonnaise**
- **2tbsp natural yoghurt**
- **2tsp wholegrain mustard**
- **1tsp grated horseradish**

1 Heat the air fryer to 160°C/325°F. Cut the swede in half and put into a bowl of cold water, to prevent it from browning, then cut into 1cm (½in) thick slices. Next, cut the slices into chunky chips. Keep them in water until needed.
2 Drain the fries in a colander then dry thoroughly with kitchen towel.
3 Toss the fries in the oil and sea salt. Air fry (you may need to do this in batches depending on the size of your air fryer) for 15 minutes, then increase the heat to 190°C/375°F and air fry for a further 5 minutes.
4 Meanwhile, make the dip by combining the mayonnaise, yoghurt, mustard and grated horseradish. Divide the dip into little bowls to serve alongside the swede chips.

Broccoli, herb & pistachio salad

Such an easy side to serve warm – perfect with roast chicken.

Serves 6 • Ready in 15 minutes

- **3tbsp Parmesan, grated**
- **3tbsp breadcrumbs**
- **Olive oil spray**

For the herb dressing:
- **Small bunch each mint, parsley and basil, finely chopped**
- **100ml (3½fl oz) olive oil**
- **3tbsp red wine vinegar**
- **1tbsp Dijon mustard**
- **1tsp sugar**
- **Juice of ½ lemon**

For the salad:
- **600g (1¼lb) tenderstem broccoli**
- **2tbsp olive oil**
- **100g (3½oz) pistachios, toasted and roughly chopped**

1 Heat the air fryer to 200°C/400°F. In a bowl, mix together the Parmesan and breadcrumbs. Make a little foil baking sheet with the edges scrunched up, spray with oil, then toast the crumb mixture in the air fryer for in the oven for 3 minutes. Meanwhile, mix together all the dressing ingredients and set aside.
2 Toss the broccoli in the oil, season, then air fry for 5 minutes, giving the bake a shake half way through cooking. You may need to do this in two batches.
3 Serve topped with the toasted pistachios and breadcrumbs.

Mexican corn on the cob

Air-frying corn gives a charred exterior with tender, juicy kernels.

Serves 4 • Ready in 20 minutes

- **4 corn on the cob, halved**
- **1tbsp sunflower oil**
- **Sea salt**
  For the sauce:
- **Zest and juice of 2 limes**
- **4tbsp crème fraîche or soured cream**
- **1tbsp Grana Padano or Parmesan, finely grated, plus extra to serve**
- **½tsp smoked paprika**
- **½tsp chilli flakes**

1 Heat the air fryer to 200°C/400°F. Rub the corn with the oil, sprinkle over the salt then air fry for 15 minutes, turning half way through.
2 To make the sauce, mix together the lime juice and zest, crème fraîche, cheese, paprika and chilli flakes. Spoon this over the hot corn cobs and top with a little extra cheese to serve.

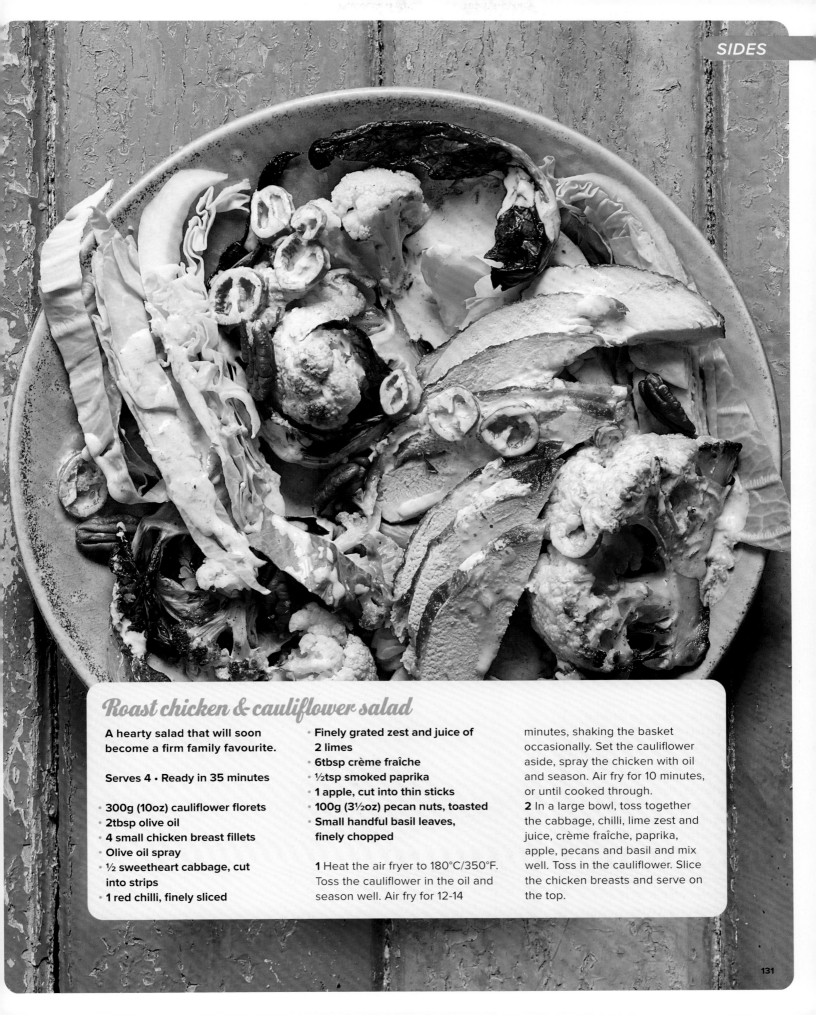

Roast chicken & cauliflower salad

A hearty salad that will soon become a firm family favourite.

Serves 4 • Ready in 35 minutes

- 300g (10oz) cauliflower florets
- 2tbsp olive oil
- 4 small chicken breast fillets
- Olive oil spray
- ½ sweetheart cabbage, cut into strips
- 1 red chilli, finely sliced
- Finely grated zest and juice of 2 limes
- 6tbsp crème fraîche
- ½tsp smoked paprika
- 1 apple, cut into thin sticks
- 100g (3½oz) pecan nuts, toasted
- Small handful basil leaves, finely chopped

1 Heat the air fryer to 180°C/350°F. Toss the cauliflower in the oil and season well. Air fry for 12-14 minutes, shaking the basket occasionally. Set the cauliflower aside, spray the chicken with oil and season. Air fry for 10 minutes, or until cooked through.
2 In a large bowl, toss together the cabbage, chilli, lime zest and juice, crème fraîche, paprika, apple, pecans and basil and mix well. Toss in the cauliflower. Slice the chicken breasts and serve on the top.

Roasted beetroot & pumpkin

You will need to cook the beets and pumpkin separately, but this lovely side dish is served at room temperature in any case.

Serves 6-8 • Ready in 1 hr

- 500g (1lb 2oz) beetroot, halved
- 2 garlic cloves, crushed
- 2 sprigs thyme
- 1tsp caster sugar
- ½tsp sea salt
- 500g (1lb 2oz) pumpkin or butternut squash, cut into chunks
- 1 handful flat-leaf parsley, leaves and stalks finely chopped
- Handful walnuts, roughly chopped
  For the vinaigrette:
- 150ml (4fl oz) extra virgin olive oil, plus extra for the pumpkin
- 3tbsp red wine vinegar, plus extra for cooking the beetroot
- 1tsp Dijon mustard

1 Heat the air fryer to 190°C/375°F. Place the beetroot, half the garlic, half the thyme, the sugar, salt and a good dash of red wine vinegar into a foil parcel and seal.

2 Air fry the beetroot for 25 minutes, or until tender. Set aside.

3 Toss the pumpkin in a little olive oil. Add the remaining thyme and garlic. Spray the air fryer basket with oil to prevent sticking, or use a silicone or parchment mat, then air fry for 15 minutes, shaking half way through.

4 Next, make the vinaigrette. Mix the 150ml (4fl oz) oil, vinegar and mustard together, then season well and leave to one side.

5 When the beetroot are ready, allow them to cool slightly. While they are still warm, use a small knife to peel away the outer skin, then cut them into quarters.

6 Add the warm, peeled beetroot to the vinaigrette and leave for 2 mins. Add the pumpkin and flat-leaf parsley. Scatter over the chopped walnuts and serve at room temperature.

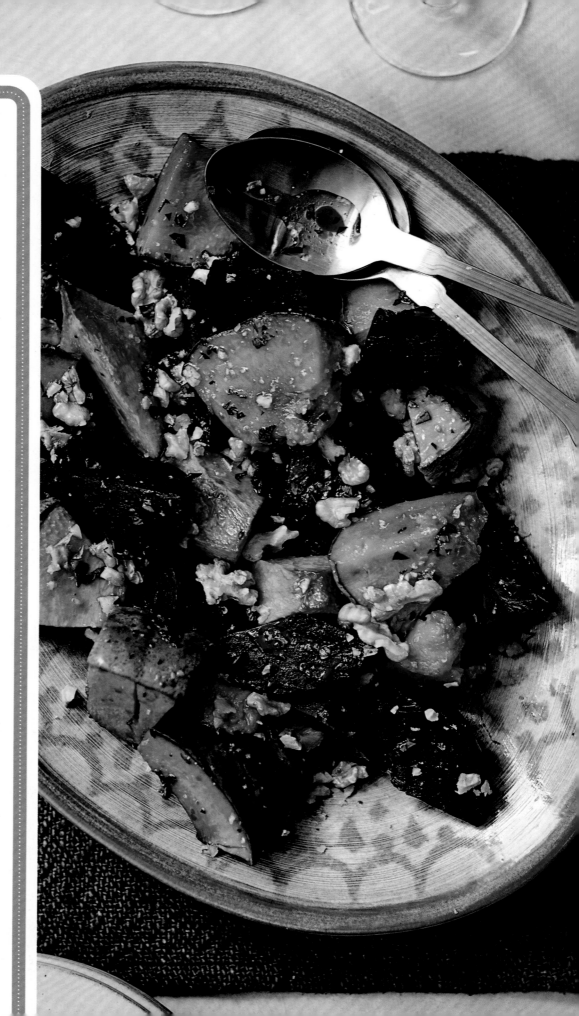

Haddock, egg & broad bean salad

Yes, you can boil an egg in an air fryer – so easy!

Serves 4 • Ready in 20 minutes

- **450g (1lb) frozen broad beans**
- **200g (7oz) smoked haddock fillet**
- **4 eggs, at room temperature**
- **2 fat spring onions**
- **30g (1oz) flat-leaf parsley, leaves picked**
- **Small bunch of chives**
- **3tbsp olive oil**
- **1tbsp lemon juice, plus wedges**

1 Boil beans in salted water for 3-4 mins. Drain, refresh under cold water, remove and discard skins.
2 Heat the air fryer to 180°C/350°F. In a pan, cover cod with boiling water and cook for 5 mins, or until flesh flakes easily. Transfer to a plate, cool slightly, then skin, bone and flake.
3 Air fry the eggs for 7 minutes, then place in iced water to cool. Peel and chop 2; halve the other 2. Mix the beans, haddock and chopped egg.
4 Slice spring onions diagonally. Roughly chop herbs, reserving a few sprigs for garnish. Scatter onions and herbs over fish and eggs. Season with black pepper.
5 Whisk the oil with lemon juice, drizzle over the salad and top with herbs, halved eggs and lemon wedges.

Roast carrots & parsnips with cumin

You'll need to cook these in two batches. To reheat, simply air fry for a minute or two.

Serves 4 • Ready in 30 minutes

- 2tsp cumin seeds
- 500g (1lb 2oz) medium heritage carrots, cleaned and halved lengthways
- 300g (10oz) parsnips, cleaned and halved lengthways
- 1tbsp za'atar
- 1 orange, sliced
- ¼tsp crushed chillies
- 4 garlic cloves
- 3tbsp olive oil
- 1½tbsp honey
- 5tbsp thick yoghurt
- 1tbsp tahini

1 Heat the air fryer to 180°C/350°F. Crush the cumin seeds gently with a pestle and mortar. Then toss them with the carrots and parsnips, za'atar, orange slices chilli, garlic, oil and honey. Season.
2 Air fry for 12 minutes, giving them a shake half way through. Remove and stir through the coriander.
3 Combine the yoghurt and tahini in a small bowl. Season lightly with salt and add a little crushed chilli, if you like. Serve alongside the roasted carrots and parsnips.

Roasted radishes with spring onions

The pepperiness of radishes mellows significantly when roasted, while the butter helps to bring out their sweetness.

Serves 6 • Ready in 20 minutes

- 450g (1lb) radishes, larger ones halved, trimmed
- 12 spring onions
- 4 sprigs thyme, torn
- 1tbsp olive oil
- 45g (1½oz) salted butter
- Juice of ½ lemon

Heat the air fryer to 180°C/350°F. Mix together the radishes with the spring onions, thyme and oil. Season well. Air fry for 15 minutes, giving them a shake now and again. Remove to a serving dish, then toss through the butter and lemon juice.

Beetroot tzatziki & yoghurt guacamole with sweet potato wedges

Sweet potato wedges are a breeze in an air fryer, ready in just 15 minutes.

Serves 4 • Ready in 30 minutes

For the sweet potato wedges:
- 3 large sweet potatoes, cut into wedges
- Olive oil spray
- 2tbsp olive oil

For the yoghurt guacamole:
- 1 large ripe avocado
- 1 tomato, chopped
- 4tbsp thick yoghurt
- 1 garlic clove, crushed
- Juice of ½ a lime
- ½ red onion, finely chopped
- 1tbsp chopped coriander

For the beetroot tzatziki:
- 100g (3½oz) cooked beetroot
- 175g (6oz) thick yoghurt
- 2 garlic cloves, crushed
- 1tbsp chopped mint

1 Heat the air fryer to 200°C/400°F. Spray the basket with oil to prevent sticking. Toss the sweet potatoes in the oil, season well, then air fry for 15 minutes, turning them half way through cooking.

2 To make the guacamole, scoop out the avocado flesh into a bowl and mash. Mix in the tomato, yoghurt, garlic, lime juice, onion and coriander. Season.

3 To make the tzatziki, put the beetroot, yoghurt, garlic and mint in a food processor and blitz until just combined.

4 Serve the dips with the sweet potato wedges.

135

SOMETHING SWEET

p*157*

Best ever brownies made in a flash!

Fruit and white chocolate muffins

Muffins bake at half the time in an air fryer. Here's where individual silicone muffin cases come in really handy.

Makes 6 • Ready in 20 minutes

- **2 medium eggs**
- **75g (2½oz) golden caster sugar**
- **3tbsp vegetable oil (groundnut or sunflower)**
- **A few drops of vanilla extract**
- **150g (5oz) plain flour**
- **1½tsp baking powder**
- **1 large nectarine, stoned and sliced**
- **75g (2½oz) strawberries, hulled and quartered**
- **75g (2½oz) white chocolate, chopped**

For the topping:
- **Half a nectarine, stoned and chopped**
- **60g (2oz) raspberries**
- **6 strawberries, hulled and quartered**
- **Light brown soft sugar, for sprinkling**

1 Put the eggs, sugar, oil and vanilla in a mixing bowl and mix well until you have a smooth liquid. Mix the flour and baking powder together in a separate bowl, then combine with the wet ingredients. Stir in the nectarine slices, strawberries and white chocolate until evenly mixed. Heat the air fryer to 160°C/300°F.
2 Fill each muffin case about two-thirds full with batter. Scatter the fruit for the topping over the muffins and finish with a sprinkling of sugar. Air fry for 12 minutes. When they are ready, the muffins should be well risen and springy to the touch.

Nutty raspberry crumbles

These are so easily rustled up. Feel free to use any frozen soft fruits, too – just thaw before cooking.

Serves 4 • Ready in 15 minutes

- **3tbsp lightly salted butter, diced, plus extra for greasing**
- **400g (14oz) raspberries or a mixture of berries**
- **100g (3½oz) caster sugar**
- **3tbsp plain flour**
- **100g (3½oz) granola**

1 Grease the sides of four deep (around 6cm (2½in) ramekin dishes with butter. Mix the raspberries or other berries with 2tbsp of the sugar and scatter into the dishes.
2 To make the crumble, put the butter and flour in a food processor and blend until the mixture resembles fine breadcrumbs. Add the granola and remaining sugar and blend lightly until the granola is broken up but still quite chunky. Heat the air fryer to 180°C/350°F.
3 Divide the berries between the ramekins and air fry for 5 minutes. Add the crumble, then air fry for 6 minutes, until the topping has browned and is crisp. Remove and allow to stand for a couple of minutes before serving with whipped cream or ice cream.

"Mix and match the fruits for these tasty crumbles according to what's in season"

139

Granola

Breakfast granola will keep for up to five days in an airtight container. Mix and match the nuts and seeds, depending on what you have in the cupboard. You'll need to air fry this in two batches.

Serves 10-12 · Ready in 20 minutes

- 1tbsp coconut oil
- 4tbsp maple syrup
- ½ tsp vanilla extract
- 125g (4oz) oats
- 60g (2oz) sunflower seeds
- 60g (2oz) sesame seeds
- 1tbsp flaxseeds
- 60g (2oz) pecans, roughly chopped
- 60g (2oz) almonds, roughly chopped
- 30g (1oz) coconut flakes
- 60g (2oz) each of dried cranberries and blueberries
- Coconut yoghurt and chopped mango, to serve

1 Gently heat the coconut oil, maple syrup and vanilla in a small pan until melted, and stir. Heat the air fryer to 180°C/350°F.
2 Line two cake tins or metal dishes with a whole piece of baking parchment. This is to avoid anything falling through the basket. Mix together the oats, seeds and nuts. Stir in the coconut syrup then divide between the two tins. Air fry for 4 minutes, stir, then air fry again for 3 minutes. Repeat with the second batch.
3 Stir in the coconut flakes, dried cranberries and blueberries. Cool in the tin then store in an airtight jar.
4 To serve, top with the yoghurt and diced mango.

Breakfast berry breads

Pushed for time? Use a pre-made bread dough or a packet mix, and scatter a little of the crushed cardamom over the fruit before air-frying. You'll need to bake these in two or three batches.

Makes 6 · Ready in 20 minutes plus rising

- 12 cardamom pods
- 400g (14oz) strong white bread flour
- 3tbsp caster sugar
- 2tsp easy blend dried yeast
- 75g (2½oz) salted butter
- 175ml (6fl oz) warm milk
- 100ml (3½oz) crème fraîche
- 6tbsp blueberry or other berry jam of your choice
- 300g (10oz) fresh soft fruit of your choice
- Beaten egg, to glaze
- 2tbsp vanilla sugar

1 Remove cardamom seeds from pods and crush in a pestle and mortar. Tip into a bowl and add the flour, sugar and yeast.
2 Melt the butter and mix with the warm milk, then add to the bowl, stirring with a round bladed knife to make a dough. Tip the dough on to a floured surface and knead for about 10 minutes until smooth and elastic, or use a mixer with a dough hook attachment and knead for 5 minutes. Turn into a lightly oiled bowl, cover with cling wrap and leave in a warm place to rise for about 1 hour or until doubled in size. Heat the air fryer to 190°C/375°F.
3 Tip the dough on to a floured surface and cut into 6 pieces. Roll each into a circle about 15cm (6in) in diameter. Put 3 circles on to a piece of baking parchment which is the same size as the air fryer basket. Spread a little crème fraîche in the centre of each, add a spoonful of jam then top with fruit.
4 Bring up the edges of the dough over the filling, pinching together to form cases, leaving the fruit showing in the centre. Brush with beaten egg and sprinkle with vanilla sugar. Air fry for 11 minutes until risen and golden. Repeat with the second batch. Transfer to a wire rack to cool slightly.

Cook's Tip
The dough can be left in the fridge to rise slowly overnight. Allow it to get to room temperature before using.

Cook's Tip

Try this with apples, too. You may need to adjust the cooking time, depending on the size and variety of apple — some are crunchier than others.

Baked pears with fresh ricotta, honey & pine nuts

This dessert may be less calorific than many, but it's just as delicious, wonderfully aromatic from the fresh rosemary.

Serves 4 · Ready in 30 minutes

- **4 just-ripe pears**
- **2tbsp honey**
- **2tbsp butter**
- **4 rosemary sprigs**
- **A squeeze of lemon juice**
- **100g (3½oz) ricotta cheese, whipped until creamy**
- **2tbsp pine nuts, toasted in a dry pan**
- **2tbsp honey and rosemary, to serve**

1 Core the pears and cut a horizontal sliver from the bases, then stand them upright in a dish small enough to fit them snugly. Drizzle with honey, dot with butter, then tuck the rosemary sprigs in and around them. add a squeeze of lemon juice and a splash of water. Heat the air fryer to 180°C/350°F.

2 Cover with foil and air fry for about 20 minutes until the pears are soft, but still holding their shape. Serve with juices from the dish, spoonfuls of ricotta, a scattering of toasted pine nuts, a drizzle of honey and a rosemary sprig, if preferred.

"Herby baked pears work brilliantly paired with a soft blue cheese"

Melting middle chocolate pots

A light chocolate sponge with a hot, ganache-like filling. Also lovely topped with a spoonful of whipped cream, which melts into the filling.

Serves 2 • Ready in 20 mins

- 60g (2oz) butter, plus extra for greasing
- 45g (1½oz) dark chocolate, plus extra for melting
- 1tbsp liqueur or spirit, such as rum or Tia Maria
- 1 egg white
- 2 egg yolks
- 2tbsp caster sugar
- Mini marshmallows or chopped nuts to serve

You will need:
- 2 x 6cm (2½in) ramekin dishes or similar, buttered

1 In a small pan, melt the butter and chocolate with the liqueur.
2 Whisk the egg white until it softly begins to peak.
3 Whisk the egg yolks with the caster sugar until it has a mousse-like consistency. With a ballon whisk, gently fold the melted chocolate and the whisked egg white into the sugar mousse mixture. Pour into the ramekins.
4 Heat the air fryer to 200°C/400°F. Air fry for 10 minutes. Drizzle with extra melted chocolate and mini marshmallows or nuts to serve.

"Chocolate fondants make such a speedy dessert, and they are always a crowd-pleaser"

Hot apricot soufflés

An elegant dessert for a special dinner. The apricots give it a welcome sharpness, so it's not too sweet.

Makes 4 • Ready in 30 minutes plus cooling

- 125g (4oz) dried apricots, chopped
- 100ml (3½fl oz) fresh orange juice
- 2tbsp single cream
- A little butter, for greasing
- 2 egg yolks
- 3 egg whites
- 2½tbsp caster sugar, plus extra, for dusting
- Icing sugar, to serve

You will need:
- 4 x 6cm (2½in) deep ramekin dishes, buttered and dusted with caster sugar

1 Combine the dried apricots, orange juice and 4tbsp boiling water in a saucepan. Bring to the boil, cover, then reduce the heat and simmer for 30min until soft and most of the liquid has been absorbed. Blitz in a food processor or blender to create a thick, smooth purée. Leave to cool, then stir in the cream.
2 Stir the yolks into the cooled apricot purée. In a large, clean bowl, whisk the egg whites with a little salt using an electric hand-held whisk until soft peaks form. Add the caster sugar and continue whisking to a firm, glossy meringue.
3 Using a balloon whisk, carefully fold the whites into the apricot mixture, a third at a time, until evenly mixed. Divide the mixture between the ramekin dishes filling them to the top. Run your thumb around the edges to create a ridge. Heat the air fryer to 180°C/350°F.
4 Put the ramekins into the air fryer and cook for 10 min or until golden and puffed up – when you slightly jiggle a dish, its contents should barely wobble. Dust with icing sugar and serve immediately.

Triple chocolate cookies

You can bake these in batches, or why not just bake a few then leave the cookie dough in the freezer for your next chocolate fix!

Makes 12 • Ready in 25 mins, plus chilling

- **45g (1½oz) milk chocolate, chopped**
- **150g (5oz) unsalted butter, cubed**
- **150g (5oz) light brown sugar**
- **3tbsp caster sugar**
- **1 egg**
- **200g (7oz) plain flour**
- **3tbsp cocoa powder**
- **1½tsp baking powder**
- **½tsp bicarbonate of soda**
- **½tsp flaked sea salt, plus extra for serving**
- **75g (2½oz) dark and white chocolate chips, or use bars, roughly chopped**

1 Melt the milk chocolate in short bursts in the microwave or in a bowl set over a pan of barely simmering water (make sure the bowl doesn't touch the water). Set aside to cool until just warm to touch.

2 Using an electric mixer, cream the butter and both sugars together until pale and fluffy. Add the egg and beat again, scraping down the sides of the bowl. Pour in the melted chocolate and stir to combine.

3 Mix the dry ingredients together in a bowl, then fold into the chocolate mixture, until no lumps are visible. Fold in most of the chocolate chips then divide the mixture into 12 equal balls. Press the remaining chocolate chips into the tops of the balls then transfer to a lined plate or baking tray and chill in the freezer for 1 hr or overnight in the fridge.

4 Heat the air fryer to 165°C/325°F. Air fry the cookies in batches on baking parchment or a silicone liner for 8 minutes, leaving space in between for them to spread. Scatter with extra flaked sea salt, if using. Leave to cool on the liner, before transferring to a wire rack.

Banana muffins

Speedy and simple breakfast muffins, best baked in silicone muffin cases. A good use for any over-ripe bananas.

Makes 6 • Ready in 20 minutes

- 175g (6oz) ripe bananas
- 75g (2½oz) light brown sugar
- 2 ½tbsp sunflower oil
- 1 egg, beaten
- 75g (2½oz) plain flour
- 75g (2½oz) wholemeal flour
- 4tbsp dark or milk chocolate chips
- 1tsp baking powder
- 1tsp cinnamon

1 Mash the bananas, then beat in the sugar, oil and the egg until well combined. Stir in the plain and wholemeal flour, the chocolate chips, baking powder and cinnamon.
2 Heat the air fryer to 160°C/300°F. Divide between 6 muffin cases – you may need to bake them in two batches. Air fry for 12 minutes.

"If you prefer a lighter muffin, use 100% plain white flour in this recipe""

Amaretti biscuits

Oven-baked Amaretti are coated in icing sugar before baking, but this makes a real mess in an air fryer, as the fan blows much of the sugar off. So we dust them once baked. They are still utterly delicious!

Makes: 12 • Ready in 20 minutes

- **1 egg white**
- **50g (1½oz) soft light brown sugar**
- **75g (2½oz) golden icing sugar**
- **225g (8oz) ground almonds**
- **Zest of 1 lemon**
- **2tbsp Amaretto liqueur**

1 Heat the oven to 180°C/Gas 4. Whisk the egg white to stiff peaks, add a pinch of salt and the sugar, a spoon at a time, while whisking until the egg white is thick and glossy. Fold in 50g (2oz) icing sugar, the ground almonds, lemon zest and Amaretto liqueur.
2 Heat the air fryer to 180°C/350°F. In your hands, roll the mixture into 12 balls. Place on baking parchment or a silicone liner and air fry for 10 minutes, flipping half way through.
3 Dust generously with icing sugar and leave to cool on a wire rack.

"Cute little Amaretto biscuits are the perfect accompaniment to an espresso"

Coconut rice pudding with fruit compote

Traditional British rice pudding bakes in half the time using an air fryer. This recipe is simply flavoured with vanilla, but you could add a little cinnamon, too.

Serves 6 · Ready in 1 hour 15 minutes plus cooling

- **75g (2½oz) short-grain pudding rice**
- **75g (2½oz) caster sugar**
- **400g (14oz) can coconut milk**
- **½tsp vanilla extract**
- **Butter, for greasing**
  For the compote:
- **450g (1lb) frozen mixed summer berries or cherries**
- **2tbsp caster sugar**

1 Butter a baking dish with a capacity of around 1.5 litres (2½pints). Sprinkle the rice into a bowl with the sugar. Give the coconut milk a good shake then pour it over the rice and stir well. Stir in the vanilla extract and pour everything into the baking dish and cover with foil.

2 Heat the air fryer to 140°C/250°F. Air fry for 1 hour, though check after 50 minutes. The rice should be tender and most of the coconut milk absorbed.

3 Meanwhile, cook the fruit in a pan with the sugar and 4tbsp water for about 10 mins until softened. Allow to cool and serve with the rice pudding.

Snickerdoodles

A soft and chewy American cookie, spiked with the gentle spice of cinnamon sugar. Bake as many as you want, then freeze the rest of the dough.

Makes: 20 biscuits • Ready in 20 minutes

- **100g (3½oz) butter**
- **60g (2oz) caster sugar**
- **75g (2½oz) soft brown sugar**
- **1 egg, beaten**
- **170g (6oz) plain flour**
- **60g (2oz) ground almonds**
- **1tsp baking powder**
- **1tsp cream of tartar**
- **¼tsp cinnamon**
  For the coating:
- **1tsp of cinnamon**
- **6tbsp caster sugar**

1 Cream butter with both sugars until light and fluffy, then gradually add egg. Stir in flour, ground almonds, baking powder, cream of tartar, cinnamon and a pinch of salt, until the mixture comes together to form a soft dough. In a separate small bowl, mix cinnamon-sugar coating ingredients together.
2 Roll tbsps of mixture into 20 balls, then roll lightly in cinnamon sugar. Flatten slightly with a fork. Heat the air fryer to 165°C/325°F.
3 Place, evenly spaced, on baking parchment or a silicone mat, and air fry in batches for 8 minutes (they'll be slightly soft, but will firm up a little once cooled). Sprinkle over extra cinnamon sugar to serve.

Apple & blueberry flapjacks

You'll need to bake these in two batches, but they are easy, very moreish and will keep for three days in an airtight container.

Makes 12 · Ready in 20 minutes

- 200g (7oz) unsalted butter
- 200g (7oz) caster sugar
- 150g (5oz) runny honey
- 425g (15oz) porridge oats
- 2 red apples, peeled and grated
- ¾tsp ground cinnamon
- 100g (3½oz) dried blueberries
- 75g (2½oz) sunflower seeds
- 75g (2½oz) Brazil nuts, chopped

You will need:
- A 15cm x 15cm (6in x 6in) baking tin, greased, lined with baking parchment

1 Melt the butter, sugar and honey in a medium-sized saucepan until dissolved, then mix until well combined. Remove from the heat and stir in the remaining ingredients, mixing well to coat evenly. Heat the air fryer to 180°C/350°F.

2 Spoon half into the prepared tin and spread and flatten to create a smooth top. Cover with foil, then air fry for 10 minutes. Remove the foil then air fry for a further 2 minutes, until browned.

3 Set aside in the tin to cool completely before turning out. Repeat with the remaining mixture. Cut into squares.

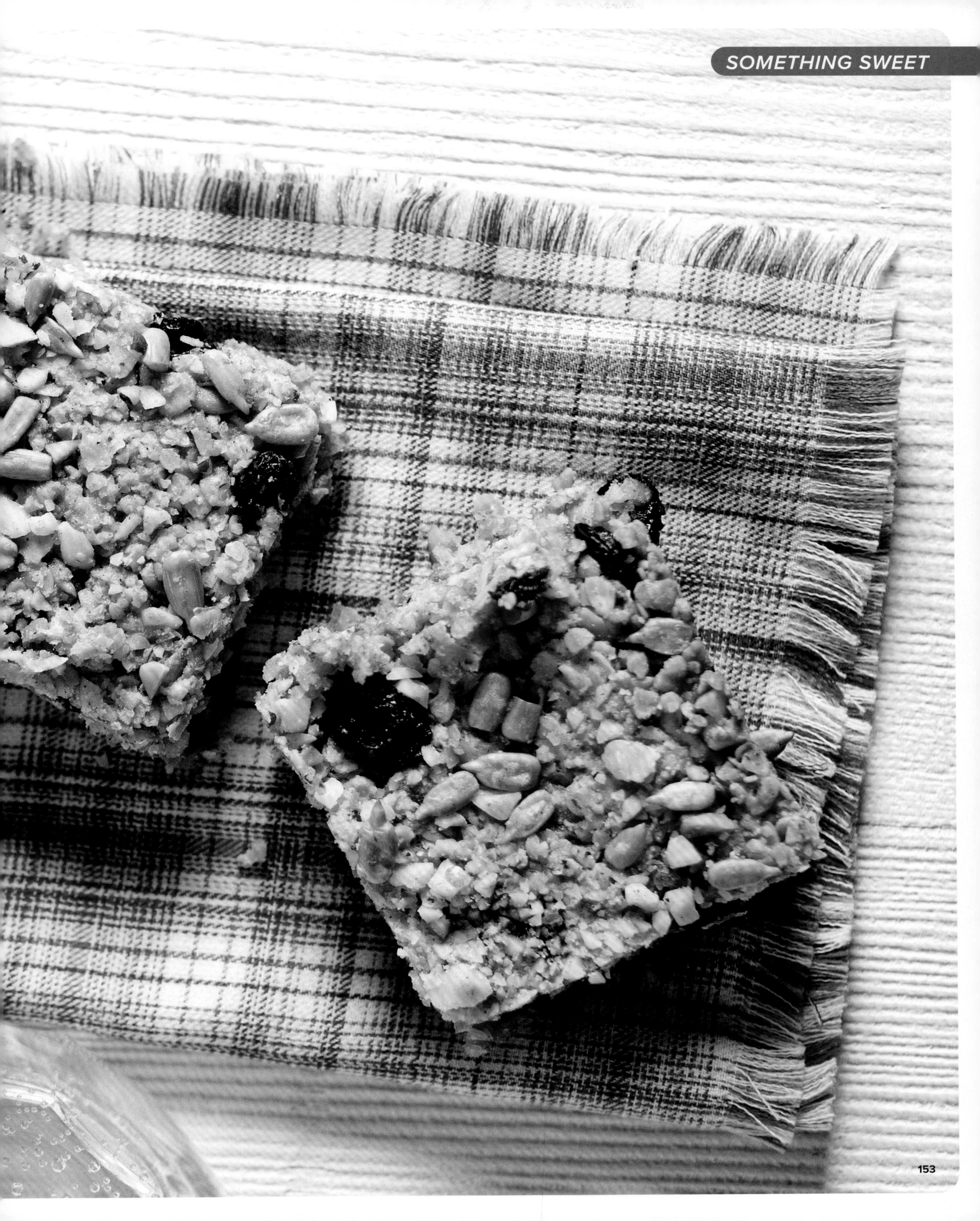

Peaches & cream scones

Scones need a light hand – an over-worked dough makes them tough and chewy.

Makes 12 small scones • Ready in 20 mins, plus cooling

- **225g (8oz) self-raising flour, plus extra for dusting**
- **60g (2oz) cold butter, diced**
- **45g (1½oz) caster sugar**
- **150ml (5fl oz) buttermilk**
- **Milk, for brushing**
- **1tbsp demerara sugar**
- **Clotted or whipped cream and peach conserve, to serve**

1 Place the flour and a pinch of salt in a large bowl. Rub in the butter, using your fingertips; it doesn't have to all disappear, a few lumps make for a flakier scone. Stir in the sugar.
2 Warm the buttermilk until steaming, then add to the flour mixture and use a table knife to incorporate. Take care not to overwork the dough.
3 On a lightly floured surface, pat the dough out to a 10-13cm (4-5in) square. Cut into 12 squares. Transfer to a parchment liner, spaced a little apart. Heat the air fryer to 180°C/350°F. Brush the tops with milk and scatter over the demerara sugar. Air fry for 10 minutes, flipping half way through.
4 Cool on a rack for 10 minutes. Split open and spread with cream and jam.

Dark chocolate & tahini cookies

You can't beat chocolate-chip cookies – unless, of course, you flavour them with tahini and edge them with deliciously nutty sesame seeds! This makes a large quantity but again, you can freeze any dough you don't use.

Makes: 24-26 cookies • Ready in 20 minutes plus chilling

- **100g (3½oz) butter, softened**
- **175g (6oz) soft light brown sugar**
- **1 free-range egg**
- **60g (2oz) tahini paste**
- **200g (7oz) plain flour**
- **1tsp baking powder**
- **4tbsp cocoa powder**
- **100g (3½oz) dark chocolate chips or roughly chopped chocolate**
- **100g (3½oz) sesame seeds**

1 In a bowl, beat butter and sugar until creamy, then gradually beat in egg and tahini paste. Sieve flour, baking powder and cocoa powder together over mixture. Finally mix in chocolate chips. Once the dough comes together, tip it out on to a clean surface and knead into a long sausage shape.
2 Sprinkle sesame seeds on to a chopping board and roll dough so the seeds stick to embellish the outside. When edges are covered in seeds, wrap dough in clingfilm and chill for 4 hours or overnight.
3 Heat the air fryer to 180°C/350°F. Remove dough from fridge and, using a sharp knife, cut into 1cm (½in) discs. Air fry on baking parchment or a silicone mat for 12 minutes, flipping half way through. They don't spread massively, but allow a little space in-between each. Allow to cool a little on the parchment, then using a fish slice, allow to cool fully on a wire rack before serving.

Gluten-free scones

They may not rise quite as much as regular flour, but the flavour and texture of these scones work just as well for a lovely afternoon tea.

Makes 8 • Ready in 30 minutes

- **250g (9oz) gluten-free flour, plus a little extra for rolling**
- **1tsp gluten-free baking powder**
- **3tbsp crème fraîche**
- **100ml (3½fl oz) pouring cream**
- **75-100ml (3-3½fl oz) milk**
- **1 egg, beaten**
- **1tbsp sugar to top**
- **Whipped cream and jam, to serve**

1 In a large bowl, mix together the flour and baking powder. In a jug, measure out the crème fraîche, cream and milk and whisk in the egg. Pour the wet mixture into the dry and mix into a soft dough.
2 Place on a well-floured surface and shape to a circle of about 5cm (2in) thickness.

3 Cut out 8-10 rounds or cut into squares and place on baking parchment or a silicone liner. Brush the top with milk and sprinkle with sugar. Air fry for 10 minutes, flipping half way through. You'll need to do this in two batches. They should be golden brown and cooked through.
4 Cool slightly on a wire rack before serving with cream and jam.

Chocolate brownies

Brownies bake in half the time in an air fryer, though you'll need to bake this quantity in two batches.

Makes 15 • Ready in 45 minutes

- **250g (9oz) unsalted butter, diced, plus extra for greasing**
- **300g (10oz) dark chocolate, roughly chopped**
- **3 eggs**
- **275g (9½oz) caster sugar**
- **75g (2½oz) plain flour**
- **1tsp fine salt**
- **100g (3½oz) walnuts, roughly chopped**
- **45g (1½oz) dried cherries or blueberries**

You will need:
- **15cm (6in) square tin, base and sides lined with baking paper**

1 Melt the butter and chocolate in a heatproof bowl set over a saucepan of simmering water. Leave to cool to room temperature.

2 Meanwhile, whisk the eggs with the sugar until pale, thick and voluminous. Heat the air fryer to 180°C/350°F.

3 Fold the chocolate mixture into the egg mix, followed by the flour, salt, walnuts and dried fruit.

4 Pour half into the tin and air fry for 15 minutes or until set on top but still slightly wobbly in the middle. Repeat with the rest of the mixture. Leave to cool then cut into squares or fingers.

"Try substituting the walnuts in these brownies for salted peanuts"

Chocolate cheesecake sandwich biscuits

These cookies are so good, even if you don't want to fill and dip them! The cookies will keep for two days in an airtight container.

Makes: 10 doubles • Ready in 30 minutes plus cooling and setting

- 250g (9oz) butter, softened
- 190g (6¾oz) caster sugar
- 200g (7oz) condensed milk
- 360g (12½oz) flour
- Pinch salt
- 1tsp vanilla essence
- 2tsp baking powder
  For the filling:
- 100g (3½oz) cream cheese
- 60ml (2fl oz) double cream
- 75g (2½oz) white chocolate, melted and slightly cooled
- 3tbsp strawberry jam
  To coat:
- 200g (7oz) dark chocolate, melted

1 Heat the air fryer to 180°C/350°F.
2 Beat together the butter and sugar. Beat in the condensed milk. Add the flour, salt, vanilla and baking powder and beat to combine.
3 Roll the mixture into 20 balls, flatten with a silicone spatula (so they won't stick). Air fry in batches for 10 minutes. Leave to cool a little in the basket, before removing to a wire rack with a fish slice.
4 To make the filling, beat the cream cheese in an electric mixer until soft. Whip the double cream into soft peaks and then fold through the cooled melted chocolate. Fold into the beaten cream cheese.
5 To assemble the biscuits, spread one with a layer of jam, top with a little cream cheese filling and sandwich with a second biscuit. Dip the whole thing in the melted dark chocolate and leave to set on a wire rack.

Mini carrot cake loaves

These mini cake loaves are extra indulgent, as a divine cheesecake frosting is tucked away in the middle.

Makes 8 • Ready in 1 hour

For the cakes:
- 150g (5oz) wholemeal self-raising flour
- 1tsp baking powder
- 100g (3½oz) ground almonds
- 175g (6oz) soft light muscovado sugar
- 2tsp mixed spice
- 3tbsp raisins
- 125ml (4fl oz) vegetable or sunflower oil
- 300g (10oz) carrots (around 3 large ones), peeled and grated
- 2 eggs, beaten
  For the filling:
- 45g (1½oz) full fat cream cheese
- 4tsp double cream
- 1tbsp icing sugar
- Zest of ½ orange
  For the topping:
- 125g (4oz) white chocolate
- 2tbsp toasted flaked almonds
  You will need:
- 8 mini loaf tins (around 7 x 9cm/2.5 x 3in), greased and bases lined; plus a piping bag (see Cook's Tip)

1 Heat the air fryer to 160°C/300°F. For the cakes, mix the dry ingredients together, then mix in the raisins, oil, grated carrot and eggs. Spoon into the tins and air fry for 25 minutes. You'll need to do this in two batches. Remove from the tins and cool.
2 For the filling, whisk the cream cheese, double cream, icing sugar and orange zest. Transfer into a piping bag and store in the fridge.
3 Once the cakes are cool, cut a deep slit into the centre of each, leaving 2cm (¾in) uncut at each end. Snip a small end off the piping bag, insert into the gap and squeeze until full of cream.
4 Melt the chocolate and spoon over the cakes. Scatter over the almonds.

Cook's Tip

If you don't have mini loaf tins, use 6 dariole (mini metal pudding basins) instead, filling them with the cream cheese frosting from the narrower top once turned out.

Coconut macaroons

Always a favourite and so quick to rustle up, with very little washing up.

Makes 12 • Ready in 10 minutes

- **1 egg white**
- **45g (1½oz) caster sugar**
- **1tsp almond extract**
- **100g (3½oz) desiccated coconut**
- **45g (1½oz) dark chocolate, melted**

1 Whisk the egg white until just firm. Add the sugar and almond extract and whisk together. Stir in the coconut. Heat the air fryer to 160°C/300°F.

2 Spoon large walnut-sized blobs of the mixture onto baking parchment or silicone liner. Air fry for 5 minutes, or until set and lightly browned.

3 Melt the chocolate in a bowl set over a pan of simmering water. Dip the base of each macaroon into the melted chocolate and return them to the baking parchment to set. Drizzle over the remaining chocolate, if you fancy.